'This is one of the best books working on bettering one's life that we are creating a produc̲ ̲ ̲ ̲ ̲ ̲ ̲ ̲ ̲ our life is overwhelmingly brillian̲t̲, ̲a̲n̲d̲ ̲I̲ highly recommend this book to anyone wanting to create a better life for themselves.'
Kelly Hoppen MBE

'Keith's life and insights are an inspiration.'
Bruce Parry, Tribe

'A flying trapeze artist, a clown, a producer of stage, screen and music and now this! Keith is a master performance coach with a real handle on the art of living fearlessly. I urge you to read this marvellous book.'
Barefoot Doctor

'A long time ago, I used to wonder: How does Keith always seem to experience and feel everything he wants? And thanks to this book, now I know! How lovely that he's chosen to share this with us, his friends, and believe me, we're all his friends.'
Nick Fletcher, senior editor DreamWorks SKG

'With so many books out there giving variations on a theme or expanding upon a solitary concept, *The Power of Raaargh!!!* is a veritable goldmine.'
Andy & Dawn Mackay, Ibiza Rocks

'In a world consumed by stereotypes and mediocrity, lives this unique individual, unaffected by the noise, gently exuding an ever-present breeze of warm spirited charm... Keith Holden, the "happiest of men," his tone of perspective strums an original tune –
*Go Cleanse Your Soul
With Rock and Roll ...*'
Andy Taylor, Duran Duran

'Consult this masterpiece for a new twist to life, and ease your mind in the face of adversity.'
Callum Negus Fancey,
The Independent's *entrepreneur 2010*

THE POWER OF RAAArGH!!!

START YOUR JOURNEY HERE

KEITH HOLDEN

HAY HOUSE

HAY HOUSE

Australia • Canada • Hong Kong • India
South Africa • United Kingdom • United States

First published and distributed in the United Kingdom by:
Hay House UK Ltd, 292B Kensal Rd, London W10 5BE. Tel.: (44) 20
8962 1230; Fax: (44) 20 8962 1239. www.hayhouse.co.uk

Published and distributed in the United States of America by:
Hay House, Inc., PO Box 5100, Carlsbad, CA 92018-5100. Tel.: (1) 760
431 7695 or (800) 654 5126; Fax: (1) 760 431 6948 or (800) 650 5115.
www.hayhouse.com

Published and distributed in Australia by:
Hay House Australia Ltd, 18/36 Ralph St, Alexandria NSW 2015. Tel.:
(61) 2 9669 4299; Fax: (61) 2 9669 4144. www.hayhouse.com.au

Published and distributed in the Republic of South Africa by:
Hay House SA (Pty), Ltd, PO Box 990, Witkoppen 2068. Tel./Fax: (27)
11 467 8904. www.hayhouse.co.za

Published and distributed in India by:
Hay House Publishers India, Muskaan Complex, Plot No.3, B-2, Vasant
Kunj, New Delhi – 110 070. Tel.: (91) 11 4176 1620; Fax: (91) 11 4176 1630.
www.hayhouse.co.in

Distributed in Canada by:
Raincoast, 9050 Shaughnessy St, Vancouver, BC V6P 6E5. Tel.: (1) 604
323 7100; Fax: (1) 604 323 2600

© Keith Holden, 2011

The author of this book does not dispense medical advice or prescribe
the use of any technique as a form of treatment for physical or
medical problems without the advice of a physician, either directly
or indirectly. The intent of the author is only to offer information of a
general nature to help you in your quest for emotional and spiritual
wellbeing. In the event you use any of the information in this book
for yourself, which is your constitutional right, the author and the
publisher assume no responsibility for your actions.

A catalogue record for this book is available from the British Library.

ISBN 978-1-84850-208-6

Printed and bound in Great Britain by
TJ International, Padstow, Cornwall.

For my amazing wife Marcela, who has shared with me the biggest lessons in my life; my two sons Marlon and Tadhg, who inspire me every day to incorporate those lessons; for Mum and Dad for the gift of life; and for Phil and Geli, both silent masters in *The Power of Raaargh!!!*

Contents

'I wonder,' he said to himself, 'what's in a book while it's closed ... Something must be happening, because as soon as I open it, there's a whole story with people I don't know yet and all kinds of adventures and deeds and battles ... Of course you have to read it to find out. But it's already there, that's the funny thing. I just wish I knew how it could be.'

MICHAEL ENDE, *THE NEVERENDING STORY*

Introduction

Raaargh!!!

Gutsy, expressive, primordial, instinctive, intuitive, spontaneous, simple... I like that so much I'm going to say it again.

RAAARGH!!!

Capturing the meaning of *Raaargh!!!* in writing is not simple. Any attempts at definition are in danger of becoming as tiresome as *'Be my friend'* and the half dozen or so other irritating phrases any talking doll might say. A doll that says nothing, however, will be cherished for years as, of course, she can say anything. Your imagination is without limits and so *Raaargh!!!* can mean anything you want.

It might be appropriate to begin by explaining why I started using *Raaargh!!!*

Ah, plenty of time for that.

If I begin by summing up *Raaargh!!!* in the Introduction, it'll be like the present trend of movie trailers that are too rushed to be enjoyable while giving it all away and making it pointless to watch the movie in the process.

Personally, I've always preferred teaser trailers, so let's just enjoy the book as it unfolds, because that is what most of us really want out of life after all.

Aside from the enjoyable element of surprise, there's this strange idea knocking about that because the Universe is infinite, every single possibility is being acted out, like an infinite number of chimpanzees with an infinite number of typewriters eventually typing out the complete works of Shakespeare. Well, we could see life in this way and consider our role to be that of a passive victim or lucky victor of random chance.

It this were the case, there wouldn't be much point to either writing this book or putting our minds to anything else. We'd do just as well to sit back and leave it to the chimpanzees. But in this frozen moment in time that I am **now** writing and the current **now** in which you are reading (the previous word *'now'* already a frozen moment in time for both of us), we are intuitively driven to take control of the typewriter and with good reason. You can do a much better job than those chimpanzees.

The typewriter is yours for the taking. Just because the script for the future is unwritten, making it literally a work of fiction, doesn't mean we can't embrace life as a work in progress and merrily type away as masters of construction in the **now**.

Life is a work in progress.

Rather than focus on the analogy of us all being authors and because I've seen more films than read books, it felt natural to construct this book the same way. The main difference between this book and any other film is that the main character is you.

Man, I'm enjoying this movie already.

Not only are you the main character and screenwriter, you are also the producer and director for this movie called *Your Life.* Regardless of your budget, all the key roles are in your hands and so the quality of the production is really down to how far you want to take it.

This creative process is happening, whether you realize it or not, and this brief spell of time, when our movies momentarily entwine, is designed to inspire you to embrace and harness your phenomenal capacity for these roles, putting your movie among the greatest stories both ever and never told.

Mass applause.

One thing I have absolutely no doubt about whatsoever is that there is more beauty and meaning within you than in any film currently receiving rave reviews and frozen on celluloid as a finished masterpiece. Any fictional tale pales in comparison to the infinite possibilities still tingling away in the NOW of all works of progress – you included.

So what benefits are in store for you, once you've taken control over your own production?

Other than the quality of your experience, one thing I promise is that I'm offering you no new benefits whatsoever.

Other than the quality of your experience, the only benefit I offer you once you've taken control over your own production is that you don't need any. You've already got everything you could ever possibly need.

Ah, but once you see it, you'll realize the best is yet to come.

Your potential is limitless.

This is the Holy Grail of *Raaargh!!!*, dangling like a carrot which can never be eaten, and driving the mechanics of all evolution. What this gem of gems means is that your process of evolution is infinite, which is why the journey is the destination, enlightenment is a pipe dream and to grow is the closest thing we have to a purpose in life.

Like a mountain climber, who thinks the next ridge is the last, once you overcome your fear of failure and success, you'll discover new pioneering fears; the exhilaration of enjoying the view right now and the knowledge you'll reach the summit, while not forgetting you've still got to climb back down again.

This is love, which if it were just support, positive thinking and mugs of cocoa, wouldn't provide the motivation for growth. Necessity is the mother of invention. Why else would you even bother to try?

The thing about necessity is it involves doing what we have to do, whereas most of us yearn for the inspiration, which comes with, or rather causes, doing what we love.

Raaargh!!! is about being and seeking at the same time.

When you have set your sights on your goal, the next step is to break down everything that appears to be difficult into lots of simple things until each one becomes as easy as falling off a ladder – providing you're willing to climb up one in the first place. This is where the momentum of *Raaargh!!!* comes in and, don't worry, there isn't any deadline.

But if life were about achieving things all the time, what a boring world it would be. Letting go and enjoying the moment is an essential part of life, too. Your process of evolution is ongoing, so you might as well say, *'Fuck the consequences!'* and have a go. *Raaargh!!!* can mean that, too.

A friend told me the motto that got him through school was, *'Just do it; it's easier to apologize than ask for permission.'* Add to this is the *Raaargh!!!* of fair exchange and it's about having the balls (or ovaries) of a train robber with a loving desire to be fair.

One thing's for certain: your movie covers all genres. A romantic- and suspense-filled historic action documentary comedy drama with numerous twists and cliffhangers, a dash of irony and inevitably a modicum of horror and disaster thrown in when you're least expecting it. Child-friendly or X-rated, accept your movie for what it is, while living happily ever after now. Hey, there's even some Kung Fu, though I've left out the zombies, but I'm not saying there isn't room to squeeze them in somewhere too, on a Sunday morning. Your life's got it all.

Hmm... So is this a teaser or an attempt at cramming it all in? Nobody said it was going to be easy, although, I guess, I did mention falling off ladders.

Let's start again and create a blank canvas.

Raaargh!!! means a blank canvas, too.

When you're absolutely certain about achieving something, it's virtually impossible for anything to stop it from happening. We all live this universal law every day of our lives. The only variable is time and how long it takes you to become certain.

Flashback.

When, over dinner, the Barefoot Doctor, a Taoist teacher and healer, suggested I write a book called *The Power of Raaargh!!!*, the certainty that I would was instantaneous and it was only the mechanics of writing that remained unknown.

There were parts I knew and parts I didn't, but the answers always came as they always do, provided I asked the right questions because, let's face it, there's an infinite number of them, too. When something didn't go according to plan, the solution was always better than the original idea. After all, what good is an idea that doesn't work?

When you have certainty and willingness to compromise, it's amazing to see how a project takes care of itself, provided you are present and prepared to action where necessary.

One thing I knew was that there are two reasons why some people are put off self-help books, for which personally I prefer the term personal growth, and the first is the misunderstanding over positive thinking.

Negativity is great!

For instance, can you think of a single movie that struck a chord with you that was negative-free? I don't believe *The Teletubbies* ever made it to the big screen but offhand I can't think of anything else. We love the concept of challenge and, more importantly, we love to see what the main character is going to do about it. Regardless of how positive your aspirations may be, you will always continue to face challenges.

Independent of our reactions to it, negative energy in its pure form simply refers to obstacles and resistance. Ask any electrician, and he'll tell you how far you'll get without a perfect balance between positive and negative.

When we try to achieve any goal, however simple, we encounter obstacles. Wanting them to go away is the surest way of ensuring they never will. Without obstacles (negativity), we wouldn't have any hurdles to leap over with an inspired vision. The fruit of our effort, along with other people's support, is the **positive aspect** of the equation, which we'd benefit from by being grateful for, but usually just take for granted.

It's the same when a plane hurtles down a runway. If it weren't for the oncoming wind resistance, the plane wouldn't have anything to push against and would never take off. Without obstacles and resistance there simply wouldn't be anything in existence to achieve!

The bigger your goal, the more engine thrust you will need.

RRRAAAAAAAAAAAAAAAAARRRGGGHHHH!!!!!!!!!!!!

And without a goal you can't score.

Everything is relative, size doesn't matter and your goals might range from becoming a multi-millionaire philanthropist to going to sleep with the lights off, and might not be anything anyone else even notices. Whatever your goals, it is working toward them which keeps you in sync with a constantly changing Universe. Not having goals makes you a passive victim of all the obstacles life will throw at you anyway.

Obstacles are neither good nor bad, though our reactions to them can certainly be pleasant or unpleasant. Negative emotions are our reactions to obstacles which we haven't mastered yet. As such, they can be a blessing because they pinpoint areas in our lives requiring attention.

When we are very young, we overcome obstacles and then move on – occasionally shelving the trickier ones – in the instinctive knowledge that we can't afford to be stuck because there is so much else we need to learn. We are no longer children and many of the lessons of an adult concern going back and dealing with the parts we didn't quite understand the first time round. The beauty in negative emotions is that they always lie, and there is always a hidden meaning staring at us, though few can see it.

The second reason many people are put off self-help books is our intuitive understanding that we are already perfect. After all, we are Human Beings, not Human Becomings, and feeling obliged to be improving or achieving things all the time takes all the fun out of life. As well as growing, our other parallel purpose in life is just to be, or rather to enjoy it.

This paradox of just being while growing is our ultimate challenge. A frivolous life deprives us of meaning, while a life with too much responsibility is difficult to enjoy.

So are we to focus on getting what we want or being happy with how we are?

The answer to all paradoxes lies in embracing both sides. Just as the best way to get what you want is by being happy with how you are **now**. The master doesn't make fundamental choices in advance, instead choosing appropriate action as the moment arises. Strength in one context is weakness in another and regardless of how similar two situations may appear, they are always unique.

A friend of mine, who was an extreme ski champion, instructed skiers by encouraging them to abandon the concept of left and right. No two turns are the same, it is one fluid line, and he taught this concept by having his advanced skiers ski blindfolded.

Use the Force, Luke.

The mysterious force...

Can you feel it?

Embrace the mystery.

Whether or not the Universe will be completely explainable one day, right now it is not and, as it appears to be infinite, it's unlikely it ever will be.

For the best results in life we must embrace the mystery while learning to distinguish between food and poison. Instead we try to explain the mystery while embracing what is poison in an animalistic desire for security.

How can there be any form of lasting security within a Universe in a constant state of change? It's impossible! The closest we can come to being in control is by accepting that one goal must always lead to another and giving up the mythical concept that everything will be OK when we reach some distant and imaginary point in the future.

No wonder everyone's insecure because we are, and it's the best part. How dull it would be if you took away a surfer's need for challenge and balance. Freedom and vulnerability are joined at the hip.

No one would attempt to strive for a goal they didn't believe was possible and yet intuitively we know we're capable of more than we are currently achieving.

Embracing the mystery is the ultimate tool for stretching the boundaries of what you believe is possible within a Universe which is infinite, so I'll say it again:

Your potential is limitless.

So far I've covered quite a lot of ground, but then life can only become easy once you've accepted it isn't. Can you imagine if life was as easy to master as a game of noughts and crosses, and nobody won, lost or learned anything ever again at all?

How mind-numbingly boring!

In the same way, chess is a complicated game and at a beginner's level it's not a question of who wins, but rather who loses. According to Fred Reinfield's *Second Book of Chess*, it is easier to learn the nine classic bad moves rather than the infinite winning variations, and then it is simply a case of not doing them. But in life, unlike chess, we are not playing to see how it all ends. Death comes in the middle of our lives – well, in one way it's the end – though most of us don't see it coming, so I guess it's in the middle.

Life can never be mastered and, at times, is frustrating as well as being the greatest game of them all. No game can do justice to the real thing because regardless of whether you win or lose, everyone is a player and...

There is no such thing as a bad move.

Mistakes are a means of learning, so remember this powerful tool of self-love next time you're tempted to feel like an arsehole because we all do, on occasions. You are wonderful and innocent, a cherished miracle of the Universe with all of time eternal to get it right through a series of actions born from *letting go*, which culminate with the realization *you need do nothing*.

So rather than talk about bad moves, I offer you the *Principles of Raaargh!!!*

While mastery of the principles comes with experience and time, even a vague understanding of them is a sufficient arsenal to help you acquire those balls or ovaries of a train robber with the loving desire to be fair.

From this point, creation is something we need only allow to happen, and understanding can only become wisdom through action. This is the final piece of the jigsaw currently unavailable in any book, including this one. This piece is within you.

So take action, and you need do nothing.

OK, that's a contradiction. Remember the skier and never bother yourself with seeming to contradict yourself again.

All paradoxes, dilemmas and contradictions exist because of the illusion that we are a separate entity to the world around us. The Universe is one entangled whole, which wouldn't be complete without you.

As such, the best way of honouring everything is through your mastery of self-expression, which can be done harmoniously with your surroundings provided you are listening.

At first, getting this balance is as challenging as rubbing circles on your belly while patting your head.

With a modicum of practice it becomes easy.

When you forget to listen, shout *Raaargh!!!*

This book is designed to show you that challenge can be as enjoyably embraceable as when watching your favourite heroines and heroes in the movies, and give you the momentum to continue when the joy isn't there, which is the real reason we admire the heroines and heroes.

Thus, the *Principles of Raaargh!!!* are designed to help you find the inspiration to embrace all challenges, which puts you in a *win-win* scenario at all times.

Enjoy the good times and embrace the bad.

This is so much easier once you understand that behind all your problems, which only exist temporarily in the physical domain, is a perfect Universe, which is relentlessly conspiring to do you favours.

The key is to have gratitude for EVERYTHING.

No easy task. Or so it seems.

To start we will work on remembering to feel gratitude for the bits that we can. For some, even this might prove challenging, but I know with absolute certainty that all you have to do is look.

Now, as the house lights are about to fade and you dive into the popcorn, in homage to universal gratitude, I can go no further without saying thank you for the invaluable help I had in writing this book.

First, I'd like to thank Johnny Golden for first enlivening me with the cry of *Raaargh!!!* and secondly but also firstly, the Barefoot Doctor for offering me, in an extraordinary act of generosity, a vehicle to embrace my own personal paradox by suggesting I write this book and introducing me to Hay House. I'd like to also thank all the wonderful people at Hay House, in particular Michelle Pilley, and not forgetting Jo, Jo, Joanna, Jessica, Steve and Amy, and Louise herself. To my wonderful editor Sandy Draper, a genius who applied her wisdom to sorting the wheat from the chaff and helped create a book I could never have produced alone, and likewise my brother Dr Phil Holden, Jamie Kelsey Fry, Anita Dhillan, Kimberley Thomas and Gill Caney for chipping in along the way. To Lorenzo Agius for the wonderful portrait on the front of this book, for

The Power of Raaargh!!!

his warmth and support and for dressing me as Elvis when I met with Hay House to pitch this book. To Kevin Palmer for shooting the promo, and Mike and Claire the creators of Manumission for letting us film in their Doctor Dolittle hideaway and the three of them for their feedback on my message, and also to Aric, Ilona and Barry and The Buddha House. To Brad Hoyland for all those movie chats we had whenever I took a break from the parts I wrote in London, and to Callum Negus Fancey for everything to date, and the joint venture we are about to embark upon. Praise and thanks to the wonderful words of Khalil Gibran, who can ground mind, body and spirit in a single sentence and whose quotes are so rife within this book. I would also like to thank Doctor John Demartini, who to date has been one my greatest teachers, and my sons Marlon and Tadhg who are my greatest students, making them even greater teachers, and my dogs Chula and Zsa Zsa who are my greatest followers inspiring to me to go for the walks where the ideas come, and if I go any further I will have to include everybody and so I will. How many seemingly unrelated incidents and people, some of whom are forgotten, contribute to making the things we do without us noticing the connection, though our hearts are filled because of them.

And finally my highest praise of all goes to my wife Marcela, without whose help this project would have been a whole lot easier, and absolutely worthless.

ACT I

'We don't see things as they are.
We see things as we are.'

ANAÏS NIN

The Birth of Aaargh!!!

U certificate
(Universal – suitable for all)

CUE – Symphony of the Universe theme tune playing to a montage of scenes from your formative years.

Roll opening titles.

Imagine your Universe as a giant orchestra playing a symphony without end, simultaneously as it being written.

When you were born, you knew absolutely nothing other than the instinct to suck. Free from distraction, you were perfectly equipped to just sit back and listen.

Ah, the harmonies!

Then, every once in a while, along came the odd bum note.

You'd become hungry and so filled your lungs before roaring a mighty,

' *Aaargh!!!* '

In need of motherly action, you turned to the wonderful gift of crying. How else would a baby ever get fed?

Reactions are absolutely essential for survival.

Mmm... good.

Mission accomplished, your attention returned once more to focusing on the wonderful music.

As you grew, you learned and en route, among all those lullabies, you encountered more and more bum notes.

So what were you supposed to do?

Turn to your only natural instinct, and carry on reacting.

'Aaargh!!!'

Distracted by the bum notes, your attention was diverted away from the music again toward the musician or instrument that dared join in with such disharmony.

'I don't want that trombone player (or whatever) in the orchestra!'

Suddenly there were more of the bastards cropping up everywhere.

'Aaargh!!!'

No fun in that.

To create balance you naturally sought *The Power of Aaahhh...* the positive reaction to pleasure and looked for something that wasn't there.

'Where's that fellow with the great big drum gone? He's my favourite and he's not here! Drums! Drums! Give me drums!'

Aversion to what you have and craving what you don't have created a dialogue of illusions, filling your mind with chatter, and leaving you unable to appreciate your present experience.

Unwittingly, with a mind full of chaos and distraction, and without even noticing, you are no longer listening to the music.

You are no longer in the here and now.

CUE – End theme tune.

Most of us are so caught up with events from the past or fears for the future that we disregard the fact that life is happening right now – this is it!

Raaargh!!!

NOW, it begins

The first scene of most films is taken up with the flavour of the main character's current life, which screenwriters refer to as the back-story or exposition. This is the dialogue and action which show the personality, disposition and current situation of the main character – whether they are a professional, have-it-all lawyer with unresolved issues about family, a teenager with a penchant for the occult or a salt-of-the-earth housewife who is overlooked by everyone; they've all got issues.

OK, some movies begin with an idyllic back-story – you know the kind of thing.

CUE – Happy family eating breakfast together, laughing and chatting, in a fabulous house.

Mind you, they are the ones who are usually oblivious to what's coming, say a meteorite hurtling toward the Earth. Well, no guesses for where it's going to land and if someone in the family is the main character and happens to survive, they've now got issues!

Well, a common goal is that we're not writing a disaster movie. It would be unfair, so let's not go there because, regardless of whatever unforeseen events may come your way, you're going to do just fine.

Possibly you're going through a current crisis or, perhaps, everything's temporarily amazing but more likely life is basically OK, though it could be better and, as in *The Matrix,* there's something missing, which you can't quite put your finger on.

Regardless of your current situation, there is one unifying factor in our lives that everyone wishes to leave behind: our negative reactions to *The Power of Aaargh!!!*

In itself, *The Power of Aaargh!!!* is no bad thing. *Aaargh!!!* is our instinctive **reaction** to fear or pain and is essential for survival in the here and now.

If your hand was over a flame and you felt no pain, the consequences of leaving it there would be a real drag. Similarly, if you were being chased across the African plains by a charging rhinoceros, any adrenaline-inducing fear would be welcomed, as it would give your sprint the edge required to make it up the nearest tree.

Fear and pain in the present are for your protection.

Nothing exists in this perfect Universe without good reason and, while it sounds all too enticing, there is nothing to gain from eradicating fear and pain completely.

The First Principle of Raaargh!!!
Everything has a place, and that place is just fine when you are present. When you're not, it doesn't seem that way at all.

Identifying Aaargh!!!

So what is the old part of your life, which you would benefit from leaving behind?

Unlike a traditional Hollywood blockbuster, this book requires audience participation as you transform from the audience for other people's movies, to the central character in your own. Once you have identified with what is holding you back, this moment marks the end of the old way of life and the rest of the script is yours for the writing.

If you want it, you got the main part, congratulations.

Raaargh!!!

Or eek!!!

For now, this is your opening scene, so let's start by studying what's happening in your current life. What would the opening dialogue and action reveal about you? What image do you project to the outside world? What fears, resentment and guilt are you holding on to? What are you craving? What are you avoiding? What is stopping you from being fulfilled?

Let's find out.

Whether or not you have a go at this exercise is up to you, but please bear in mind that this is not a positive visualization of how life will be in the future. Instead, it is designed to help you identify the cravings and resentments which are preventing you from listening to the symphony.

Studying the scene of your present life and identifying negative emotions, which are holding you back, may not seem helpful now but by the end of this chapter you'll be on your way to eliminating the *Aaargh!!!* and discovering your goal.

And that's a promise.

Raaargh!!!

✳✳✳ EXERCISE ₁ ✳✳✳

Get horizontal.

Close your eyes and focus on your breathing, however it is, for a short time before imagining every part of your life you don't like.

Fill your mind with all the chaos in your life and create an Act I opening scene which surpasses anything you have seen in any movie. Think of your version of that trombone-playing bastard who has wronged you, and the obstacles and or people preventing you from achieving a rosy future.

What outside forces are stopping you from getting what you want?

What is causing your fear, anger, guilt or resentment?

If focusing on these obstacles evokes strong emotions, then *Raaargh!!!*

So how do you feel?

My guess is not great.

Sorry about that.

The point is, how are you going to achieve anything feeling like that?

A negative visualization may not seem appropriate, but among your positive aspirations, when you're low, don't you end up beating yourself up and doing this exercise without being asked to anyway?

This exercise is designed to make you conscious of what you are doing in order that you can begin to act out of choice. Next time you find yourself doing this, say to yourself, 'I don't need Exercise 1.' If you're too stressed to continue, take a deep breath, go and make a cup of tea and come back because this is where the nourishment starts.

Negative emotions are artificial

The cravings and aversions you experienced in Exercise 1 for things to be different only result in making you feel bad. What is more, they are artificial because they are feelings you are having in the **present** for events which are **not actually happening** at the same time.

Guilt and resentment are based on memories of the past, just as fear (other than from present danger) is based on your projections of the future, and they don't bear any connection to the music that the symphony of the Universe is playing now.

Take comfort in the fact that your negative emotions always lie and a friend that sometimes lies is way harder to predict than a friend who always lies; treat your negative emotions accordingly.

The Second Principle of Raaargh!!!
No thought, logic or conclusion that stems from a negative emotion is true.

///

At the exact moment you are expressing *'Aaargh!!!'*, the sensations within you are the loving effects of the Universe shouting, *'Raaargh!!! Oy, you! Forget all that, look over here and become present.'*

So, in the immortal words of The Sex Pistols:

'NEVER MIND THE BOLLOCKS!'

We can be so busy focusing on what happened in the past or projecting the future, we forget that neither of these realities is happening now. Negative emotions, created in the past, are turned into labels – such as ugly, clumsy, careless, talentless and so on – which we use to define ourselves in the present. Blinded by our negative emotions, we forget that the **future is unwritten** and **our potential is limitless**. You cannot label or constrain something without bounds.

Not convinced.

To help illustrate this process, let's skip to a behind-the-scenes documentary to find the source of *Aaargh!!!*

Universe = energy = you: *One Love.* It is a scientific truth that the Universe is one unified field of energy which is constantly changing, transforming in shape and form. All living organisms, including you, are part of this energy.

Energy can't be created or destroyed. The sun gives energy to plants, which transforms into the energy of life and growth and provides a source of food, which we eat and burn off and, in turn, we give off heat into the air and ground, and on and on. We are all part of this infinite chain of energy.

All matter, including our physical bodies, is made from pure energy. Your body is made up of cells, which are made of molecules, which are made of atoms, which are made of subatomic particles. The deeper you delve, the more you find only energy, where there is no difference between nouns and verbs because what they're made of, as well as what they're doing, is one and the same.

An apple is made up of pure energy. For the apple to have the appearance of matter, it is made of tiny particles of energy, which, for some unexplainable reason, maintain a relationship long enough for us to consider the apple as a solid entity. The particles of energy within the apple are most certainly not stationary. On the subatomic level they are not only moving at phenomenal speeds, they are also constantly disappearing into thin air as new particles take their place.

So while in actuality an apple is a temporary manifestation of a constantly transforming swirling mass of energy particles, labelling that phenomenon as an apple, let's face it, is rather handy.

Labelling can be useful in the right context. As we grow we accumulate knowledge that is absolutely essential for our survival. The green round thing over there is delicious, nutritious and called an apple, whereas the berry over there is poisonous and will kill me if I eat it. We apply labels to momentary pockets of particle energies in order to draw from our memories for information without which we couldn't possibly survive.

But a successful life is one that achieves a balance between heart and mind.

We just looked at how energy in form of particles enables us to label nouns such as apples. At a subatomic level, energies take one of two forms – not just particles, but also waves.

In actuality, all energies exist in an infinite state of wavical possibilities, which was first highlighted by the English scientist Thomas Young in his groundbreaking experiment in 1801. The Double-Slit experiment showed that photons (light particles of energy) behaved as waves when we weren't observing them and as particles when we were.

Well, so what?

Well, while *the Power of **Raaargh!!!*** is infinite, *the Power of Aaargh!!!* is entirely graspable. Once you can understand the nature of energy as waves and particles, which make up you, you can see the meaninglessness of limiting yourself with unnecessary rigid particle labels for something that is ever transient and based on the past and future. It also means you can tap into the realm of possibilities in the now where your potential is limitless.

(Roll credits)

INTERMISSION

It is at this very point, during the book's first ever read through, that my wife stopped me and said, 'Darling it's getting a bit heavy here. Why don't you tell one atom to tell the other atom to f@*£ off?'

I suggested she write the sequel book, Living with the Power of Raaargh!!!

Written by Marcela Lopez Holden, release date tbc.

Well, OK, Marcela you've got a point, though to throw the ball back, as we're both accustomed to doing, please consider the French mathematician Henri Poincare who wrote:

'The scientist does not study Nature because it is useful; he studies it because he delights in it, and he delights in it because it is beautiful. If Nature were not beautiful, it would not be worth knowing, and if Nature were not worth knowing, life would not be worth living.'

Unlike Poincare, I'm not a scientist and, in addition to beauty, I've jumped on the wavical nature of infinite possibilities because it is a very useful piece of information indeed. Once you understand *The Power of Aaargh!!!* on the subatomic level, the gem of gems comes through understanding that all problems only exist in the physical domain. In the quantum/spiritual domain of **actuality** there are no problems away from the distracting illusions of *reality* (limited to only the parts we can realize), which is where you truly exist.

This understanding is one of the many tools of *Raaargh!!!* which will enable you to transform problems into challenges and challenges into manifesting the movie (your life) of your own design.

Besides, if you can get your head round this part (which I'm certain you can), the rest of the book will be a total laugh.

Remember that the beginning of a movie involves an old part we wish to leave behind, which can always be a bit heavy, while the true Power of Raaargh!!! is still waiting for us. Skip to it by all means, though I find the ending of a movie only has an impact if you've watched the whole thing, while the key magical elements of alchemy may be hiding in whichever parts appeal to you the least!

So back to apples, waves and particles!

It is not difficult to imagine how wave-form energies relate to our lives when you think about the joys of listening to music or experiencing an orgasm.

Our true link between our consciousness and the Universe is via a kaleidoscope of wave-form sensations. With time we label these transient sensations as *I'm too hot; I'm too cold; I'm hungry; I'm full up* and the old favourite, *my nappy needs changing, and I mean now!*

The emphasis on our sensations changes from focusing on the wave-form sensation to labelling the particle aspect of the noun, say an apple or the poo in our nappy, to create our reality and ultimately understanding of what we're going to do about it.

The only thing preventing us from accessing our infinite potential is blocks, and all blocks are illusions caused from exactly the same source.

The blocks are created when we react to transient wave-form sensations, stemming from challenging events, and apply fixed particle noun labels to them; this confuses our reactions and opinions, and creates negative particle matter from our emotions, gravitating us downwards.

Well, OK, that's a bit of a mouthful, but in essence labelling an apple is useful, whereas labelling apples as being bad, or worse yourself or somebody else as stupid, causes blocks.

Well, whoopee we can get rid of all that.

To demonstrate, I'll share a memory or two from my own childhood.

When I was at nursery school, the government supplied milk for every child. One day I remember feeling sick and didn't want my milk. The well-meaning teacher didn't agree – I still remember the feeling of being force-fed that milk. The result was that I threw up the milk later over my loving Mum.

No surprise, when Margaret Thatcher cut back on the milk in 1971 earning her the title *'Thatcher, Thatcher, the milk snatcher'*, it was all well and good with me.

I still can't drink unflavoured milk but fortunately I ended up labelling the milk, not the teacher, as being the problem, or Margaret Thatcher as my saviour. There was no connection between my illness and the milk. I had applied a particle label, separate from the unified Universe of interconnected wave-form energies, which had no relevance or benefits whatsoever.

This follows Heisenberg's Uncertainty Principle which, among other things, states that the *'observer creates what they observe'*. I didn't create the concept of milk, but my experience created my negative associations with it.

Our collective aim is to find the truth. Certain aspects of our reality are shared and others are unique to everybody. Labelling a piece of fruit is useful, whereas labelling milk as being the cause of my illness was not.

My aversion to unflavoured milk was immediate, but often we'll have no actual memory of the source of our *Aaargh!!!* and, until we identify the problem, have no way of overcoming it.

For example, according to my mum, I was an angelic child until I went into hospital for a week just before my second birthday. I can still remember being wheeled into the operating theatre and the smell of rubber when I was anesthetized. When I came out of hospital I was not the same angelic baby at all and became what can best be described as a handful.

Twenty or so years later, I was well aware that my life had a very creative and yet destructive path. With the help of dream therapy, I discovered I had been dreaming about this childhood experience without ever making any connection to it. Our dreams are the attempts of our subconscious mind to bring our attention to something we're ignoring. Before I understood the source of my *Aaargh!!!*, I was so in denial that I turned all sense of vulnerability upside down and ran full on toward my fears with no regard for self-preservation. In hindsight, as all challenges are also springboards, it turned out to be no bad thing. Why else would I have thrown myself onto a stage as a circus clown, performed as a flying trapeze artist and am now writing this book?

Meditation practice refers to such incidents as sanharas. There are three levels of sanharas. The first is like running your finger through water and creating a groove, which is quickly and automatically flattened; the cause of the incident is quickly forgotten. The second sanhara is described as chiselling a groove in wood; the incident may be worn away by time. The third level of sanhara is likened to chiselling a groove into stone; the memory remains engrained. Third-level sanharas create strong associations and are usually formed in our formative years. In adulthood, these experiences can dominate and result in inappropriate automatic reactions, without any knowledge whatsoever of their link to a particular incident.

Our greatest feats are often born from our third-level sanharas, just as flowers grow well in manure. If only we could see all moments in time simultaneously and stand in awe at the divine order of the Universe.

Ah, but there's plenty of time for that.

While there are so many different paths, it is important to note that you can transform a third-level sanhara simply by focusing on separating your sensations from reactions, which can be achieved through Vipassanā Meditation. Understanding the source of your *Aaargh!!!* gives the benefit of choice when those negative associations try to trigger an automatic negative reaction.

I don't profess to be a healer but I do know that the sanhara of most relevance in preventing you from achieving your goal is the label of *I can't*. While you can't staple jelly to a tree, for all those things you **really** care about:

Raaargh!!! I can!!!

I can't is caused by the weakness of *(u)hhh*. *(U)hhh* is stagnation and, while it can prevent a burnout, it can also prevent us from leaving our comfort zone and facing our negative emotions. It's easier to say *'I can't'* than do something about it.

Did you know that a domesticated adult elephant could easily pull the stake out of the ground to which she's chained but, remembering her days as a baby, it never occurs to her to try? As a baby *I can't* was true but saying *'I can't'* as a reaction to a negative emotion in an unconnected moment in time is stagnation.

You can return to listening to the symphony of the orchestra of the Universe and master the instrument, but **you can't manage anything you are emotional about**, which is the only prerequisite of incompetence.

Disregarding the negative labels you have accumulated and realizing they are illusions, which don't apply now, means **you can manage your emotions**.

The labels we give ourselves or adopt limit our concept of reality and our potential. Imagine fancying someone and he or she turned round and laughed at us. It is something we don't want to hear from a revered source and, feeling vulnerable, we take them seriously.

We regard ourselves by an ever-expanding list of both positive and negative perceptions or labels derived from other people – our parents, siblings, teachers, friends, and on and on – ultimately joining into this process and doing the same thing to ourselves and, like the full-grown elephant, never realize we can pull out the stake and free ourselves of these limitations.

I can run, but I'm not any good at team sports.

I'm thorough, but I can't be creative.

I'm passionate, but rubbish in bed.

I'm looking for love, but I'm ugly.

Nature cannot be defined or labelled. Even the nature of an apple can be questioned, and yet labelling it is helpful. In contrast, labelling yourself *ugly* is naming an entity which cannot be defined or judged. Another person's perceptions of our talents or appearance originated in the past and we apply them to our present, which is a new and unique event. Labelled like particles, adjectives such as ugly, stupid and clumsy take on the properties of matter, making the power of *Aaargh!!!* a concrete *reality.*

Beauty is in the spirit and the spirit is always transient. We are all ugly and beautiful in perfectly equal proportions and in a kaleidoscope of forms. It is only our thinking that can be beautiful or ugly and, like our perceptions about the world around us, it is transient and changes by the second. Think about it; *I love my job/I hate my job* can be separated by as long as it takes to drink your morning coffee.

But if we've read the label one too many times, no amount of reassurance of our beauty can penetrate the impregnable wall of separation we have built around ourselves. Dr Stephen Wolinsky discussed this point brilliantly in his book *Quantum Consciousness*, and writes in great detail how **part**icle *consciousness is* a**part** *from the Universe around us.* In other words, to see yourself as isolated and separate from the world is the root of all problems, which only exist in the physical domain of separated individual objects.

Aaargh!!! But I'm still fat!

Labelling yourself is a self-fulfilling prophecy. Beauty is not only in the eye of the beholder; it is in the mind of everything which is beautiful. Feeling fat or ugly or stupid pins a label on yourself, which everyone else can read. If your illusions appear to be reaffirmed by the reactions of others, then it is because they are simply reading your label.

The beauty of realizing that you are made of energy and not labels or other peoples' hapless perceptions means that **you can** begin to harness the power of *Raaargh!!!* **You can** realize your limitless potential to transform your destructive energy into constructive and **you can** tap into your primordial intuition of what you know to be true.

On the other hand, if you go into the world feeling ugly, clumsy, fat or stupid, then the likelihood is that the perception of you from others will follow accordingly. Telling yourself *'I'm useless'* or *'I'm clumsy'* usually results in behaving in a way that mimics your label.

Life is a mirror

If I go to a bar where I live, in Ibiza, for a *café con leche* with the mindset of *I'm a foreigner,* there's absolutely no question that the bartender will seem to be unwelcoming. *Café con leche*, no frills.

If I go into the same bar thinking, *Yay, people!* the same barman will invariably look into my eyes and smile, adding a suitable salutation. Although, interestingly, if I go through the motions and smile for effect, he'd recognize me for an approval-seeking foreigner before

I even open my mouth. The world is a mirror reflecting whatever you're feeling.

Just like looking in the mirror and seeing your reflection, this process is instantaneous. Our collective interactions are as finely tuned and immediate as a flock of starlings flying in one swirling and beautiful wave, so forget the idea of karma, as inappropriate choices, made in the past, are more likely to govern your way of being in the now, which **can** be reprogrammed.

Yawning, laughter, sadness and insecurities are infectious. Imagine having a great time with someone and, as you parted, they told you they had a great time. In return you want to express likewise but your nervousness imparts you are simply going through the social motions. The other person detects your insecurity and reflects it back at you. Although, if you do create the wrong sort of mirror, it's worth remembering that just as labels transform quickly from productive to counterproductive, the reverse is also true.

It is also worth noting that we aren't starlings. If you feel great and it's not reflected, don't take it personally, as the other person is probably preoccupied. Perhaps they are contemplating a part of their own particle consciousness which has nothing to do with you, other than, yes, you were doing exactly the same thing as they are now about a half an hour ago.

Transforming destructive to creative

Affirmations work in the same way as labels and for that matter hypnotism or NLP (neurolinguistic programming) techniques and, if used wisely, can transform your energies or feelings from destructive to creative.

Changing your automatic reactions requires repetition, repetition and more repetition until the affirmation is absorbed by your subconscious mind and becomes an automatic reaction.

So what is it you want to affirm?

Let's take a completely miserable individual, which let's face it could be all of us occasionally, and imagine that he or she started using the affirmation *I am happy...*

What does that mean?

After all, the Buddha said that the search for happiness is the 'root of all suffering'.

What? The pursuit of happiness is surely what it's all about?

An ongoing form of happiness requires an ongoing form of harmony with *whatever* is happening, which means not basing our happiness on events which we label **good or bad**. Searching for happiness is as frustrating as ripping the house apart to find the car keys when all the time they're in your pocket – and look at the mess you've made in the process.

How would an oppressed blues musician of the 1930s have got on if they had sung a jolly good tune about how happy they were?

> *I woke up this morning*
>
> *Doh de deh do*
>
> *And everything was great!*
>
> *Doh de deh doh do*

The whole reason those dudes sang about what a totally rubbish time they were having in the most miserable of fashions was to create a meditative trance. The music evokes feelings or waves that create a trance, which is detached from negative associations and able to transform into anything. The blues are not sung to make anyone depressed; they are intended to create bliss.

This isn't re-labelling; this is getting out the scissors and cutting off the label.

This is **Raaargh!!!**

Art that evokes sadness is not attempting to depress you; it is cathartic and attempting to liberate you. Has the sorrow of a film or piece of music never fuelled your tears and given you an overwhelming awareness of the beauty of it all? It is these moments, along with seeing your newborn child for the first time, which give us a glimpse of what it is to open our hearts.

If you are at rock bottom in your current opening scene, then that's as good a place as any because it means the only way is up. The renaissance was preceded by 100 years of plague and wars, so know that time always has great treasures in store for you as we are all learning how to get it right.

Labelling what we think are the causes of our joys and sorrows will lead to the opposite feeling. This is the reason why spiritual teachers and philosophers talk about suffering being the path to the truth, although enough is thrown at us without needing to give ourselves a hard time too. I am not saying you shouldn't strive for things that make you happy. The affirmations and the tools in this book are designed to help you live in harmony with the present and transform negative emotions, but also know that the worse you feel, the greater the liberation you are about to experience and don't doubt it for a single moment.

If you take nothing else from this book, at least know that the divine order of the Universe means that wherever you are right **now**, you have the potential for greatness just as the most beautiful blooms grow in shit. Don't miss out on the experience of liberation, which is just around the corner.

When you're low, try this exercise and you will see that a renaissance is possible. It's coming.

EXERCISE 2

This blues transformation is dedicated to a dear friend who jumped under a tube train last week. The loss of his life is devastating and his renaissance is the inspiration he has left behind not to do anything so stupid.

I love you, Alistair.

Get horizontal.

Focus on your breathing, however it is now, for a couple of minutes.

Close your eyes and select the cause from Exercise 1 which provoked the most highly charged negative emotions.

Focus on it until it consumes you completely.

Once you are consumed, divert your attention from the negative causes to the physical

sensations those emotions have given rise to in your body.

Now focus only on those sensations.

The particle nature of these sensations will have manifested a fixed physical form somewhere in your body, such as perhaps a tight sensation in the shape of a triangle in your chest.

Keep focusing on the form of these sensations, as the associated cause behind it begins to drift away out of thought.

Keep focusing.

Without association, the fixed shape becomes a transient wave. Feel the shape begin to move and flow, and follow it wherever it chooses to go.

Keep going until you reach a state of bliss.

Don't short-change yourself with this exercise.

You deserve it.

Take some time afterwards to reflect.

Remember to try this exercise the next time you are naturally stressed, heartbroken or bereaved.

The story so far...

Act I was a scene depicting the current aspects of your life in need of change, followed by a glimpse of a life without the dominance of the power of *Aaargh!!!* – the cry of reaction to negative emotions. If you can't manage your emotions then you can't manage anything, and the means of managing them is the knowledge that they always lie.

It goes without saying that life is transient, sometimes up and sometimes down. At times it can feel like we've been dealt all the wrong cards which can dominate our ability to write the future. As you become the scriptwriter of your destiny, recognize that you can navigate this transience, while tuning into the symphony and appreciating your present experience; and this is happiness.

Negative emotions can be put to wonderful use. In fact they are doing this already, but for now repeat the following affirmation until you feel it with certainty, and then repeat it some more. Once you've read the book, choose the affirmation you feel is most useful for you as you begin your journey. Repeat it to yourself as often as you can, until you see it is exactly how you are living, and adopt the other affirmations when they become appropriate.

AFFIRMATION

I transform my negative emotions into the most powerful tool to understand the hidden meaning and opportunities of my current situation.

The Raaargh!!! of Thanks

Well, thanks for still being here.

A life full of gratitude is the foundation for everything, and I don't mean receiving it. If all you want is for people to thank you, just go around saying, *'You're welcome,'* and 98 per cent of people will automatically give you the reply you're after, and you can skip the rest of the chapter.

Goal!

Goals are the Plot Point 1 of your movie.

The Third Principle of Raaargh!!!
If you don't have a goal, you can't score.

Plot Point 1: your defining moment

This is the event in any film that gives the main character a goal to aim toward. As I have absolutely no idea what your goal may be, I'll keep it impersonal and illustrate Plot Point 1 with the ridiculous. In so doing, I want to reaffirm that you are the main character in your life, I am the main character in mine – putting us both into a stronger position to contribute to anyone who may be dependent on us – and this is a book.

So let's digress away from your movie as much as possible, which is why I'll choose the movie with the meteorite and the happy family to demonstrate Plot Point 1.

As it turns out, the happy family wasn't without some degree of turmoil. Our main character gets into an argument with his kid sister Tammy over her irritating talking doll. His parents, as always, take her side, so he throws down a bread roll and storms off, taking his loyal dog Lassie for a moonlit walk in the forest.

On hearing an explosion, he rushes home to discover it wasn't a meteorite at all, but an alien spacecraft. As there is no sign of aliens, he sifts amongst the rubble in a fruitless search for his family. *Don't worry, they'll be fine!*

Lassie growls at a shadow so our hero picks up a charred baseball bat and runs in that general direction, only to be interrupted by the sound of Tammy's screams. He stops in his tracks as his head turns quickly in the direction of his sister's voice and, with renewed determination, he runs toward the spaceship just in time to see a lanky version of E.T. dragging his kid sister inside. Just as he reaches the ship, the doors close and it flies away. Looking down, he finds Tammy's favourite talking doll. He pulls the string on her back and she says, *'There's no place like home.'*

He looks up to the empty sky and shouts, *'Aaargh!!!'*

The pain in his eyes *(which took 147 takes to capture)* transforms into absolute determination and certainty.

28

He doesn't know how but, there's no question, he's gonna get Tammy back.

Raaargh!!!

The Universal Plot call to adventure: gratitude for challenge

As I said earlier, necessity is the mother of invention. Maybe for you right now – as it is for all of us at some point in time – your current situation is a means of survival. Or perhaps you have an inspired glimpse of how your life could be and know what would or will be your dream role. Either way, having a goal requires an acceptance of the job in hand, even if with reluctance.

We can do better than that.

Unlike movies, our lives are a series of never-ending tasks and, rather than keep you in suspense or work together on finding your current Plot Point 1 for your particular movie, this book has a Universal Plot call to adventure, which is common to all of us, all of the time, and which links the paradox of being both a Human Being and a Human Becoming. I want you to transform all doubt into determination to acquire this Universal Plot Point 1; it is the tool of tools for all other tasks to which you can screw your courage.

The more you try and take on board, the more likely it will end up being a temporary fad. Some books promise so much, as does the blurb on the back of this one. My Zen Yoga teacher once said to me, at the end of a ten-day retreat, to only try and incorporate one new thing into my life which I had learned there. And there is one thing which incorporates everything in this book and it is the Universal Plot Point 1 that I want you to take away with you.

Are you ready?

The Fourth Principle of Raaargh!!!
Be grateful for challenge.

Gratitude is everything

Gratitude is the ultimate state of presence because, unlike negative emotions, you wouldn't want to change a thing. So when you consider the paradox of all philosophies on whether to focus on being happy with how you are or getting what you want, **only in those moments of gratitude for challenge are you fulfilling both.**

Think about it for a moment.

As an old man, the twentieth-century French novelist Marcel Proust wrote that while all the good times were wonderful, they were meaningless, as all the substance which had made him a great writer was the result of the misery and obstacles he'd gone through and ultimately overcome. This sentiment is echoed in all forms of art and acts of greatness throughout time and reminds us that, as the poet Kahlil Gibran said so eloquently, *'When you are joyous, look deep into your heart and you shall find it is only that which has given you sorrow that is giving you joy.'*

When things are going your way then it's easy to feel gratitude, but when they're not you feel out of sync with the Universe and consumed with negative thoughts. Don't wait until the time has passed to realize your most supreme moments and achievements arise when you are most challenged; **generate gratitude now**.

Gratitude for challenge is the most efficient path to achieving all other goals, and **if you don't have a goal, you can't score**.

I used to believe balance was the most powerful tool to access the life you want. But balance what? There are so many areas you can work on balancing, whereas gratitude immediately puts you in a state of harmony with the Universe and right smack, bang in the middle of the here and now.

Before embarking on the great quest of what you want in life *(on which you are already)*, it will be born from whatever you have available to you at the moment. What you appreciate, appreciates in value, and what you don't – whether it's a partner, a business, a car or your health – depreciates, and it's that simple.

Having nothing to be grateful for is a state of mind. Why would the Universe entrust you with something you are likely to neglect? Universal law is all about the fact that whatever applies to the Universe applies to you. So what would you do if you were the Universe, which for all intent and purpose you are?

If you went to a lot of trouble to buy the perfect gift for someone and they sneered at it, would you be in a hurry to give them something else? Only grandmothers are that wonderful, so if yours is still around, make sure to give her a massive ***Raaargh!!!*** when you open that beautifully inappropriate new addition to your wardrobe.

The Fifth Principle of Raaargh!!!
Be grateful for absolutely everything.

Thanks in abundance

I found myself slightly peeved this morning and not feeling remotely like writing a chapter on gratitude. I picked up the nearest book, which happened to be *It's Not How Good You Are, It's How Good You Want to Be* by Paul Arden, and opened it at a random page. And guess what? It said that we all get blocks and suggested looking out the window and making whatever catches your eye the solution to the problem.

So I gazed into the garden and, perhaps it was the serendipity of it all, but I immediately spotted a cactus. *What a happy-looking chap.* Sometimes all it takes is to guide the mind somewhere else, just as a puppet can distract a child from a grazed knee.

We can feel gratitude for absolutely anything. It's easy, just as it's easy to empty our minds of ingratitude for our present life. Look around you and you'll see the evidence of millions of years of evolution and the blood, sweat and tears of our ancestors who made everything possible for the life we lead today. Movies, guitars, spoons, medicine, farming, books, cream cakes, contraceptives, Botox, Christmas, dishwashers and pretty much anything else you may hold dear today came from them.

Thank you.

Gratitude is fundamental to everything.

Gratitude expands beyond yourself and naturally creates interaction with the world around you, whereas blame, resentment and guilt turn you inward and imprison you within the confines of your solitary thoughts.

Have you ever noticed that when you're unhappy you generally think of yourself? Any energy spent focusing on being a victim isolates you and literally throws away your power to have any degree of control over your own life.

Gratitude, on the other hand, expands outward, like a wave of energy, allowing you to connect to everything around you NOW. Gratitude gives you control of your present experience.

Can you think of a single example when you experienced resentment or guilt for anything while it was actually happening?

Fear, pain and anger, perhaps, but blame, resentment and guilt come afterwards, which means we spend huge chunks of our lives being preoccupied by events that are simply no longer happening. Although, by regurgitating them into the present and applying them to inappropriate situations, we're pretty good at keeping these automatic reactions alive.

Let go! Now!

Feeling gratitude for the world around you, whatever has happened in the past (even if is was five minutes ago), creates a blank canvas within where you can find inspiration in order to create wonderful things without.

Am I repeating myself?

Good.

Resolving external sources of resentment

Last week, I saw the wonderful movie *Despicable Me*. The main character is an arch villain who adopts three kids as a means of helping him. Inevitably, he ends up abandoning his path of crime, opens his heart with gratitude and becomes a loving father. My son was ready to hit the fairground at that point, whereas under my 3D glasses my eyes were full of tears.

Transforming deep resentment into gratitude requires a modicum of work, but there is one thing you can do right now to stop reinforcing the barriers on a heart closed to gratitude. Reconsider all those scenarios we moan about, with which we don't have any personal involvement whatsoever. For instance...

...the news. When I moved to Ibiza, my good intentions of keeping up with events at home fell by the wayside as I read nothing and rarely watched TV. The only time I did was on trips to London, where I was shocked by stories of rape, murder and teenage stabbings, which seemed to be everywhere. This was truly a scary place and I felt glad we'd left, and yet London felt so normal when we lived there...

A few weeks later, I watched the documentary *Bowling for Columbine* which, in its search for meaning for the mass murder of students by two fellow student gunmen, posed the question: what is the cause of the phenomenally high rate of murders in the USA?

Many believed it was the availability of guns, but the number of guns per person is even greater in Canada, and they have one of the lowest murder rates in a first world country. They then looked at the differences in the media. The US media focuses on terrorism, car jacking, rape and murder, whereas Canada's focuses more on the elderly, the health system and education.

The evidence is not conclusive but it was worth a try so I experimented with not reading the newspapers, even when I was in London. Instead, I chose writings and movies which inspired me and comedies like *The Mighty Boosh*.

My experience of London changed, too. Encounters were as warm and welcoming as they are everywhere, providing that was my mood also.

Just as which food you put in your body has an enormous effect on your health, so information can have an enormous effect on your state of mind. I'm not suggesting avoiding current affairs, but choose wisely. Be an active citizen, but concern yourself with areas you can do something about, which is ultimately everything, but only providing you have freed yourself from the restrictions of resentment and fear. Dictators can only gain control of a country gripped with fear, so if the state of the world concerns you, and with good reason, don't moan about it – get involved.

It is very difficult to cultivate gratitude for a world presented as it is on the news. Go to the Notting Hill Carnival in London and see a million happy people celebrating life, or stay at home and be thankful you didn't go when you read about the single act of violence, which would have probably happened anyway.

...com-blaming (the act of complaining and blaming).
Sources of resentment are not just created by the headlines, as much as the mindless blaming of others

about the most trivial of matters – whether they are soap stars, movie stars, royalty or your neighbours. *They, they, they, bloody they* have nothing to do with your life right now. The more you fill your mind with finger-pointing literature, the more likely you will live among a constant backchat of *Well, did he now?* and *Oh, she never!*

This type of mindless chitchat enforces a reality of blame while distracting us from living in the present. Com-blaming about anything we haven't directly experienced re-enforces the belief that nothing is our fault and that therefore we have no control over events. Gratitude for what you have means taking ownership of your life and experiencing life as it happens.

Raaargh!!!!

...mindless criticism. Another great feeder for blame and resentment is talking ill of other people behind their backs. While many people would be mortified if caught criticizing someone behing their back, on the TV show *Big Brother* the contestants quickly acclimatize to the cameras and steam into the most vicious of back-stabbings. Have you noticed the winner is usually the person who joined in the least? This seems to reaffirm the old line that whenever you are pointing the finger at someone else, three of your other fingers are pointing at you.

Next time, even if it's your worst enemy that comes up negatively in a conversation, defend them, don't join in, or say as my wife does: *'Darling I'm at a party and you're spoiling my fun. I really don't want to know.'*

It's funny but the things we think about most are the ones we hold of highest value, even if it's with resentment or blame. This means that any logic which springs from these feelings is valuable energy used to justify why you can't do the thing you'd love to do most. Go on YouTube and look at someone's film of a cover song by one of his or her heroes. Unless they're super good, most of the comments will be abusive. These comments represent the fears people have of having a go at something they'd dearly love to do.

Don't underestimate the effect mindless criticism can have in preventing you from doing the thing you love.

Generating gratitude

So to start, let's look at replacing all this mindless rubbish with being grateful for the parts we can. There is no question that, regardless of your state of mind, you can call upon memories or events for which you can be grateful.

✳✳✳ EXERCISE 3 ✳✳✳

Write them down.

Memories don't exist except for when they are brought into the present tense. Bring your memories into the present by writing them down.

Get a book of blank paper and list everything for which you can possibly be grateful. A wonderful toy you were given at Christmas when you were a child, the smile on Granny's face when you unwrapped that appalling sweater, the time a teacher was kind to you, a movie which made you cry with joy, your dog's wagging tail when you come home and absolutely anything else you can possibly think of.

Write them all down.

My list is on my computer and when I get even a vague inkling of being hard done by, I look at it and am immediately overcome with a sense of warm and present thanks. A book is even better as you can carry it with you, glowing and resonating with the giddy glee of the present of presence at all times.

Once you're in the habit, just looking at a cactus can snap you out of feeling resentful.

Be grateful for your body.

Be grateful for having the courage to pick up this book.

Hey, I'm even grateful for my wife.

This exercise is worthy of becoming a life's work.

Start it right now by recalling every memory you possibly can that you are grateful for, until you either smile with uncontrollable joy or weep with the beauty of it all.

IF YOU DID THAT EXERCISE THEN YOU'RE READING THIS IN THE HERE AND NOW.

Raaargh!!!

Gratitude is magic: use it

Gratitude is a state of presence where you wouldn't change a thing.

Only now do you have the ability to create anything, or rather transform anything, out of what you already have and love. These are your ingredients and tools, whether energy or matter, from which you create your movie, and your future will be the result of how present you have been.

Gratitude gives you the ability of an alchemist and a magician, producing miracles which others, and even you, may take for granted simply because they take longer to manifest than pulling a rabbit out of the hat.

> **'Most people think of magic as the subverting of natural laws. However, real magic does not subvert anything. Magic is merely the result of directing the creative activity of the Spiritual (Quantum) world into the material plane.'**
>
> **MARK HEDSEL, *THE ZELATOR***

Not much chance of that happening if you're unhappy with your lot. Believing you've been lumbered with crap ingredients means you'll be unlikely to produce the rabbit.

There is no such thing as crap ingredients. There is a weakness in every strength and a strength in every weakness, and com-blaming about lead will never turn it into gold.

The very stuff you resent is the gateway to your dreams.

Make the weakest point an advantage. It's always there if you look for it.

Imagine what you could achieve if you were grateful for absolutely everything.

Every challenge is worthy of welcome because your true destiny lies in what can be achieved once you've overcome it. Only when you have gratitude for challenge can you find inspiration and enthusiasm, which is simultaneously the most and least obvious path to everything.

Creating a state of gratitude

So how can you be in a state of gratitude if you were dealt a really dodgy hand? And what exactly is the definition of a dodgy hand? Without question this is our greatest challenge.

Your negative emotions lie, so there's no question that any blame, resentment and guilt hold an element involving you, which you're overlooking. This has nothing to do with blaming yourself, as all of us are constantly acting to the best of our understanding in our worthy pursuit of happiness. It is about taking responsibility, the ultimate position of self-empowerment.

Focusing on the negative aspects in others will mean you won't identify with those elements in yourself, and therefore will bring them with you into another relationship or situation and blame them (or yourself) inappropriately again and again and again. Have you ever wondered why you were attracted to these people in the first place?

A teenager told me recently of how he felt frustrated because his mother was always trying to change him. It never occurred to him that arguing with her about her trying to change him was attempting to change her; he was mirroring her frustrations. When he stopped reacting, so did she.

I love it when they get it quickly.

The obstacles of others can either be a cause of resentment or the greatest lessons and source of gratitude imaginable.

The ultimate tool for self-growth is time, as we increase our level of understanding within it. Aim to have these benefits NOW. Only a state of gratitude for both support and challenge can achieve this.

'I suggest we learn how to take anything bad that happens to us and polarize it. Instead of being overwhelmed by a negative event, dodge to the side like those T'ai Chi guys and let it whiz by your pants. Maybe it makes a little breeze – big deal. (Please, don't mistake this for optimism.)'

FRANK ZAPPA WITH PETER OCCHIOGROSSO,
THE REAL FRANK ZAPPA BOOK

The subplot: gratitude for fear

What's fear got to do with gratitude?

Well, let's not forget that I've borrowed the structure in parts from the movies and, as one of the supporting characters in your movie, allow me to indulge myself. Fear is our subplot.

I love a good subplot. They allow us to dodge sideways.

Fear is wonderful, and I am most certainly not without it.

Fear is nature's protection and lets us know when it's time for change. Animalistic fear in the here and now is exclusive to anything which can be a possible threat RIGHT NOW. Fear produces a huge instant burst of adrenaline, helping us think faster in order to decide quickly whether it's time for fight or flight, at which point we can punch harder and run faster.

Animals are truly in the here and now but I wouldn't swap what comes with our capacity to understand for anything. Where it gets more complicated for human beings is our capacity to apply fear to situations that aren't happening **now**. Instead, we make projections about the future, as well as changing the emphasis from situations which we want to get out of, to situations we'd prefer to get into.

Asking someone out on a date, or the boss for a raise, can become so important to us that not taking action becomes crippling. Instead of the choice between fight or flight, it becomes the choice of whether to avoid it or not.

Understanding fear is attempting to point out areas in your life and which you need to empower creates another source of gratitude. Gratitude for fear guides you toward it, empowering your gut instinct to know what to avoid, which in no way is the same thing as running away from something of which you're afraid. Ignoring fear is not an option, while suppressing it can lead to delusions and imbalance.

The Sixth Principle of Raaargh!!!
Unless your gut instinct tells you otherwise, always proceed toward your fears.

It is the plummeting downwards on a rollercoaster with fear for our lives that creates the elation as we hurtle up out of it. Proceeding toward our fears, as in all adventure tales, is symbolic to have died only to be reborn with new understanding.

I don't recall ever being as afraid of anything as much as my first flying trapeze show. I was comfortable with the moves but had never performed in front of an audience, with lighting and music, so had no idea if they would change my reference points causing me to miss and break my neck. In the nights leading up to the show I dreamed about the stunt where someone caught my feet going wrong. The ten-minute call to show time felt like an hour and a half and, busting for a pee, I went every 90 seconds, producing about four drips each time.

*Feel the Aaargh!!! and then shout **Raaargh!!!***

The show was another matter. *Wow*. Performing was about as here and now as I've ever been and almost comparable with the birth of my sons.

I'd pushed my comfort zone and any fear for later shows transformed into tantalizing excitement.

Now, I'm not suggesting you take up a dangerous sport as an antidote for vulnerability, though be my guest.

If not smoking cigarettes makes you insecure then embrace insecurity.

If there's a possibility you'll have to get up and talk in public about the book you're writing, then book a date for the biggest talk possible.

If you're afraid Dolce & Gabana would never take your new concept seriously, then hunt for their number.

If the person sat opposite you on a first date fills you with insecurities, then great; it means you're not indifferent, so keep going.

If you're afraid of making a mistake, then remember that the person who doesn't make mistakes is unlikely to make anything, so keep going as the worst thing that can happen if you do is that you'll find yourself in the same position as if you don't.

Resolve your fears, one by one, and keep on going.

Blame, resentment and guilt, all stem from imbalanced perceptions we have from self-justifications we made when we didn't keep going. Once you understand that any *mistakes* you have made were love in the form of challenge for the person on the receiving end, you never need to apologize or feel guilt ever again.

So how about that really dodgy hand?

All of us have or have had something so challenging it's impossible to imagine taking responsibility for it, never mind appreciating it. When you find gratitude for these moments, the feeling of enlightenment is beyond any other experience imaginable. While we have these moments to some degree throughout our lives, wouldn't it be great to pull up our largest elephant stake in just a matter of hours?

So do you want the good news or the bad news?

The good news is that I know the most powerfully consistent method on the planet for achieving this.

The bad news is that I didn't invent it; Dr John Demartini did.

Bollocks!

Quantum Collapse. Demartini is a leading authority on human behaviour and personal development. The technique Demartini uses to help people to overcome fear – and those third-level sanharas, if meditating for prolonged periods doesn't sound enticing – is the 'Quantum Collapse Process', which he describes in his wonderful book *The Breakthrough Experience*. You can also attend his *Breakthrough Experience*; this is significantly more expensive, but Demartini's certainty and ability to delve deep into the truth beind our negative emotions makes it worth every penny.

So what exactly is this process?

Oh, I can't tell you. Go and buy the book and if that pisses you off then that's more love in the form of challenge.

What I will tell you is that you pick a person you have an imbalanced perception of, ideally with resentment, which, of course, turns out to be you.

I saw people on the Breakthrough Experience who had been dealt the worst of hands. In a room full of more than 100 people, every single person broke down with tears of gratitude from the realization that undoing those events would also take away something far more precious.

At the end of the process, you pick someone in the room that somehow represents the person you're collapsing as an opportunity of thanking him or her. I was picked as someone's father who became my son, then by someone who was collapsing himself *(the most fascinating of exchanges!)*, as well as turning into someone for the person I'd picked out myself, as the whole room swirled with the actuality that **we are all one**, transforming in and out of different forms.

A perfectly balanced universe. Demartini is fond of the view held by many physicists that everything is made of light. But even if you don't accept this view, the nature of particles and antiparticles works in the same way in regard to being positively and negatively charged. Particles have an associated antiparticle with the same mass and opposite electric charge. This means that the Universe is perfectly balanced between positive and negative electrical charges, right down to the smallest building blocks from which everything is made.

The way Demartini applies this to the practical understanding of love is fantastic because, according to this principle, the dualities are perfectly balanced between pleasure and pain, support and challenge, war and peace, praise and blame. At the exact moment you are being blamed, you are being praised. Absolutely everyone and everything, right down to the subatomic level, is receiving a perfect balance of love in its two forms of support and challenge. This also sheds insight as to why there is no difference between good and bad events. There are only events, which appear good or bad when the mind looks at them with an imbalanced perspective.

Addictions and infatuation arise when something is regarded as having more benefits than drawbacks; resentment and guilt when something is seen as having more drawbacks than benefits. There are never more positive or negative aspects to anything because the number of negatively and positively charged photons is always equal in every single aspect and element of this entire Universe.

Universal gratitude

The world is a mirror and so the Universe creates order out of chaos at every single possible level and showers us with gifts of support and challenge in perfectly proportioned packages. It is only our individual consciousness, lacking the luxury of the full picture, that needs to catch up, which as we are and always will be a work in progress is absolutely perfect too.

So, why think positive?

Negative thinking exists in order to rid us of our addiction to positive thinking. The *bad* stuff are simply areas that we haven't understood yet, while all our greatest achievements, the ones we wouldn't change for anything in the world, were born out of overcoming challenges, which at one time we may have labelled *bad.* Why don't we just ignore people and situations that are a pain? We are attracted to them because they are our biggest teachers, which if it wasn't for the resentment, we'd never have had the opportunity of realizing. Once the lesson is learned, we are no longer attracted to the destructive aspect, and on it goes, becoming easier and more rewarding with every step.

Strengths and weaknesses. Have you ever noticed that strengths and weaknesses are the same thing, determined by the context not the content? Even ice cream doesn't taste good if you've just eaten three tubs of the stuff.

The single-minded courage, vision and determination of a CEO suddenly become arrogance and recklessness when the deal doesn't come to fruition.

The admiration for someone who speaks his or her mind becomes the resentment that this person never seems to know when to shut up.

The nagging to keep the house tidy becomes the joy of living in a better environment.

The loathing of discipline becomes the pride of great results.

'He's so easy going!' *'He's so easy going!'*

'She's so assertive!' *'She's so assertive!'*

'It's so decadent!' *'It's so decadent!'*

This balance of positive and negative is evident in the natural world, too. Yosemite in California, USA, is one massive plate volcano which explodes like clockwork every 600,000 years, taking 98 per cent of life on the planet with it, and it takes 20,000 years for life to recover.

How awful!

Or is it?

Aside from the fact that new, more evolved species are given the opportunity of running the roost for a while, if our planet wasn't volcanic, it wouldn't be magnetic. This means no life could ever come into being as it would be cut to pieces by radioactive cosmic rays before even having the chance of becoming a twinkling in a father's eye. The Earth's magnetism repels these rays and all life is free to thrive. So what's the odd reshuffle every 600,000 years for immortal beings such as ourselves, whose atoms were once in shooting stars and dinosaurs, compared to never having existed at all?

After all our sun is middle-aged and will inevitably explode, taking our planet with it. Is that awful? Is that the end?

Of course it isn't!

When you can see the divine order of the Universe, your heart opens with gratitude that everything is perfect in an endless here and now. There is no such thing as *good* and *bad*.

Good and evil. All events can be separated into what the person responsible intended and the effect these actions have. They are not the same thing at all.

We have already looked at how negative emotions

always lie or, as Ouspensky said, how they arise from *'artificial centres'*. The fact that our negative actions are automatic, mechanical reactions means we are innocent – at least, from our own perception. The only way you could describe something as a sin would be if you had an understanding of what the alternative would be. And if you did, you wouldn't do it.

We are all innocent.

Imagine an incident, such as someone spilling your drink, flirting with or insulting your partner. The incident gives you a choice to:

<a> Ignore it.

<b> Get red in the face and shout, *'Did you call my bird a pint? Let's have it!'*

<c> Other.

Choice b isn't really a choice; it is an automatic reaction.

So, how do I know? I know because if instead you went:

<1> Incident

<2> Deep meditation

<3> Choice,

it would be absolutely impossible to choose option b and you would be able to choose what happened next.

Creating choice. Meditation – the act of becoming present and focusing on your breath – creates a blank canvas within and gives you the opportunity to choose, whereas negative actions aren't choices at all; they are automatic reactions. Automatic reactions are necessary, as in the case of dangling your hand over a flame, but when deciding whether or not to get involved in a punch-up, they limit the human potential to the same as that of an animal, which has virtually no choice at all. Regardless of the paths we take, everyone is driven by the pursuit of happiness. Even if someone is doing something they believe is fundamentally wrong, they do it because they believe that if they don't, they won't be happy.

When we are unhappy we think of ourselves, whereas when we are happy we automatically act with compassion. If someone is ultimately selfish and wants lasting happiness, the only way of obtaining it is through compassion for others.

This means that acts we describe as wrong or evil must involve a lack of understanding at some level.

Viewing understanding about good and evil in terms of black and white is to live in a world in which, as the old saying goes, *'It's good when I sleep with your wife but it's bad when you sleep with mine.'*

Think in terms of hot and cold, rather than black and white. Temperature relates to measuring the amount of movement of molecules. The slower the molecules move, the more we describe it as cold. The coldest temperature called absolute zero is the point when molecules are motionless. The more molecules move, the warmer it gets. A burn is the damage caused when molecules move faster and faster, rather like a series of tiny high-speed molecular car crashes.

Yet when someone leaves a door open we say, *'Oy, you're letting the cold in!'* No, they're letting the warmth out. There is no such thing as the force of cold; it's a description for a lack of molecular movement and we draw the line between hot and cold depending on our own comfort, which is different for a lizard as it is for an emperor penguin. Just as the cold describes a lack of movement, what we describe as evil acts are the result of a lack of understanding and, though I don't deny its effects can be devastating, ignorance is not an absolute force.

The only absolute is the force of love and the minimum level of understanding required is to know that love comes in perfectly proportioned quantities of challenge and support. Although it may not appear this way when we react to individual pieces of the jigsaw puzzle, unaware of the full picture. I call this...

Pronoia. The constant conspiracy of the Universe to do you favours!

Transforming gratitude

So what of children with leukaemia and holocaust victims? Nothing puts people off learning Universal Law more than these injustices.

We are all innocent and these injustices were never the result of punishment. Writing about this subject is ridiculously inefficient, I'm sowing a seed. Even if you reject it, don't react as we look for common ground.

We've already looked at Vipassanā, the Ferrari of meditations, and I'm reminded of a lesson from S.N. Goenka, which I will apply here.

He said that understanding spiritual teachings is like going to a restaurant.

When we first take our seats, we read the menu to decide what to order. This is the first stage, in which we read great teachings with no idea of whether they are any good. The second stage is debate, as we look around the restaurant toward the other tables to see and smell the dishes, and determine whether the food here looks any good. This is a uniquely human capacity as we choose what to accept and reject. But if we react, we limit our capacity to being like a dog and never get to find out what the ambrosia – which for Goenka comes through meditation – actually tastes like. One thing of which I can assure you is that you can never capture the experience in a book; it can only come through your own experience.

The Universe and everything within it is absolutely perfect as it is. It is only our consciousness that needs to catch up, which as we are and always will be a work in progress is absolutely perfect, too.

It would be lovely to think I wouldn't change a thing when I read this book in ten years' time, but it's unlikely. There's no difference between the reader and the writer because all of us are **a work in progress**. Be my guest to reject anything in this book that takes your fancy. But don't react.

I remember when I first encountered another difficult concept, which was the idea that my love for my children was selfish; it just incensed me with anger. In time I knew it was true and my love for my children became more constructive than ever.

So it goes.

> **'Your children are not your children. They are the sons and daughters of Life's longing for itself. They came through you but not from you and though they are with you yet they belong not to you.'**
>
> **KAHLIL GIBRAN**

For now, know that the truth will come to you but only when you're ready to see it. The past, like sin and karma, doesn't exist. There is only **now** and the areas in need of empowerment.

The collective consciousness is perfect now. If you could see through the eyes of every single being simultaneously, you would see this is true, so make it your ultimate goal while living in the physical domain.

> **'He no longer saw the face of his friend Siddhartha. Instead he saw other faces, many faces, a long series, a continuous stream of faces – hundreds, thousands, which all came and disappeared and yet all seemed to be there at the same time, which all continually changed and renewed themselves and which were yet all Siddhartha ... He saw all these forms and faces in a thousand relationships to each other, all helping each other, loving, hating and destroying each other and become newly born.'**
>
> **HERMAN HESS, *SIDDHARTHA***

Conclusions

As the chapter draws to a close, I want you to realize that you have everything you need right now. I'm not talking about fame and fortune, as both are by-products of the thing you are most inspired to do. I'm talking about what are the benefits you would gain should your dreams come true? Personal freedom, self-expression, or whatever it may be for you. This is not a creative visualization exercise. This is recognizing current actualities for which you aren't grateful now because they are occurring in forms you aren't acknowledging and spread across different aspects of your life. Don't expect them to come in one complete package. The perfect partner who ticks all the boxes can only come along once you have the gratitude, which means knowing the boxes are already ticked by the different people currently in your life. Once you are certain they are there, it is impossible not to find them, and the more you react, the longer it will take to see.

Lead and gold are both metals, each with equally distinct qualities, whether you choose to recognize them or not.

Nobody can produce gold without gratitude for the lead.

More importantly, every aspect of yourself and your life is already perfect – always has been and always will be. The only flaw is those moments when you don't realize it, which only exist to give you the reason to look.

Open your eyes.

So what's all this got to do with Plot Point 1?

Well, everything.

You are as absolutely perfect as the Universe in which you exist. Your version of reality is like a movie completely within your control but your movie is not as great as it could be. Pretty much all movies begin with the part you are leaving behind. In this book, it is the end of the dominance of artificial negative emotions, which contain a hidden meaning.

You could dedicate your life to meditation, yoga and the way of the Sufi, monk or nun. But there is another way.

You don't have to separate yourself from the world to find hidden meanings when all you need to cultivate is **gratitude for challenge**. The world is yours for the taking, but if you're not grateful for it **now**, then you won't be when you get what you think you want, and so will be no better off. You have everything now and defining your goals gives you an inspired glimpse of how your life will be once you realize it.

In no way are your goals the same thing as cravings. Craving involves dissatisfaction with the present. Your goal is to be grateful in the present not only for what you already have, but also for the challenge of what you aspire to become.

You can co-exist as a Human Being and a Human Becoming because that is exactly what you are doing right now.

AFFIRMATION
My whole being is consumed with gratitude for EVERYTHING RIGHT NOW.

The Script

'The future is unwritten' wrote Joe Strummer...

Hang on a minute, is there a glitch in the matrix or have I used that line before?

OK, let's change it.

The Seventh Principle of Raaargh!!!
Write the future down.

The written script is a physical manifestation of your goals and aspirations and serves as a stepping stone to creating whatever it is you want.

The Universal Plot Point 1 of having **gratitude for challenge** remains as you write because regardless of what you do, life will continue to throw obstacles at you.

So what obstacles do you want to be grateful for?

You may as well know that the obstacles being thrown at you exist in order to achieve your dream role, rather than any old obstacle for any old bit part that may crop up.

By now, I hope that Plot Point 1 is at the forefront of your mind.

If you don't have a goal, you can't score.

You are the scriptwriter.

You are a master.

Go for it.

Write it down.

If you have absolutely no idea what your dream role is, then write down: *'I want to know what my dream role is!'*

That's a pretty cool Personal Plot Point 1.

If you have an inkling of an idea of what you want to achieve, write it down.

What is the Plot Point 1 you can aim for with determination?

Get out that typewriter, although an old biro and the inside of a cornflakes packet will do.

Better still, put it in a cherished book, or a computer.

Put it somewhere where it won't get thrown away as this is your future we're talking about here.

The more detail you include, the more material you're going to have to work with.

You can make a bad movie out of a great script, but you can't make a great movie out of a weak one.

There is no affirmation at the end of this scene because the future is unwritten, and everything's yours for the writing.

ACT II

'The whole punk ethic thing was do-it-yourself, and I've always been very literal, especially as a kid. When they said that anybody can do this, I was like, "OK, that's me."'

MICHAEL STIPE

The Raaargh!!! of Obstacles

Act II is known as Conflict.

In Act I we got a taste of the main character's life and found out what goal they have, need, desire, choose in order to score.

As you're working from your script now, let's well and truly establish what goal you'd love to score.

In terms of your movie, once your heroine or hero knows what it is they'd love to achieve, it's the job of the scriptwriter to throw obstacles in their way to make it as difficult as possible to achieve it. You know the kind of thing: finally found the perfect partner but turns out they're married.

Next!

Many a script never even gets read because it's clear, within the first few pages, that the writer is preoccupied with the wild and wacky events the main character has to endure rather than with resolving the plot.

Nobody cares.

The reason we watch movies is because we're only interested in what our heroine or hero is going to do about them; we're only interested in characters who take action. Try and think of a movie where your hero reacts to the power of *Aaargh!!!* with...

DONNY
Err... I just can't be bothered.

Meanwhile, the audience, which includes us, yearns to see situations resolved.

So perhaps it's now my job to have fun and throw as many obstacles at you as possible. Well, that would be kind of unfair.

Regardless of what you and I both do, life is going to throw obstacles at you anyway, so why add to them? Well not just yet anyway. Besides, I'm not the scriptwriter, you are.

Without a script, all obstacles come when you are least expecting them and need to be dealt with as an act of survival, while the smaller ones are greeted with reluctance and get shelved, building up a backlog to give you a real whammy later. The simple act of planning your goals is a means of acquiring something you love and putting you in control to deal with anything else which comes along in the process.

Obstacles and opportunities are the same thing, just as the Chinese word for *'crisis'* also means *'opportunity'*.

Hmm...

The purpose of obstacles

Obstacles exist in order to serve you; they are our incentive to think, have or do something we don't already. Obstacles work in the same way as physical discomfort: they point us in the direction of our needs; take them away and you wouldn't know your needs any more. If your only goal is to remove discomfort, the Universe will bombard you with a barrage of the stuff as an act of love to guide you to open your eyes, because that goal is both pointless and impossible.

Raaargh!!!

Have goals and accept it's probably going to get rough on the way. If you want your wagon train to make it to California, you're going to have to get through the mountains and deserts while being shot at by Indians.

Where's your sense of adventure?

Know your true goal

My wife did a lot of positive visualization when pregnant with our first child. Birth is a painful experience and she was instructed to visualize it as a beautiful one. When the midwife said a couple of days before the birth, *'Ya bebies too big. It's gunna beya caesarean,'* my wife flipped. She turned down so many treatments and the suffering she experienced was extraordinary, matched only by her phenomenal resilience. Her 'natural birth' lasted three days, before the doctors took over and gave her an emergency caesarean.

Of course it was all worth it in the end and we're all still living happily ever after, except for when we're not. It's just that this wouldn't have happened had she aimed high and compromised. Her true goal was our son, the most positive of all manifestations, not the birth itself, but it's worth being prepared to deal with whatever might happen.

Be prepared for anything.

You can handle it.

By the way, our second son was an elective caesarean and a full night's sleep was had by all. Whatever works to achieve your goal.

Optimism

Essayist and philosopher Alain de Botton made a TV series called *A Guide to Happiness,* which for each episode picked an ancient philosopher who could be of some benefit in the modern world. The third episode featured Seneca on Anger.

Seneca was a tutor and advisor to the Roman emperor Nero who, according to history, was a crazed psychopath responsible for the burning of Rome in a feat of megalomania and anger. So Seneca had his work cut out for him and attempted to resign twice in an act of self-preservation. As both requests were declined, he had no choice other than to put the teachings from his book *To Novatus on Anger* to the test.

For the TV show, de Botton applied Seneca's teachings to a road-raged, blood-vessel-bursting, London-based white van driver.

The driver said that the cause of his anger was the traffic and bad drivers. Seneca would have told him that his problem lay in the fact that he was an optimist.

You what?

Well, clearly the driver was anticipating a day with no traffic and a road full of drivers who would give way with a smile. Alain de Botton told the driver to spend a few minutes before setting off by imagining how bad the traffic and all those other drivers would be.

It worked. The driver didn't curse any more and every time he found a clear road and a considerate driver it was a bonus.

In no way is this idea contradictory to having positive goals. Positive aspirations are all about the outcome being positive, and short- and long-term benefits are not the same thing, as any recovered heroine addict will tell you.

Make your goals positive and understand that negativity is an act of love to put obstacles in your way in order for you to achieve them. Obstacles are blessings; they are opportunities to gain something you need, which you currently don't have or do.

Open your heart with gratitude to the divine order of things.

In the meantime, if you are currently shouting at people to '*fuck off*' on a regular basis, then you might want to consider experimenting with pessimism for a while.

Overcoming I can't

Apart from wars and famine, the only thing ever stopping anyone from achieving their goal is the feeling of *I can't*. Here lies the root of all obstacles. The conflict is never with the obstacle.

The conflict is with you.

Nothing is difficult. Being an expert involves knowing lots of simple things and then putting in the time to improve your skills.

When I grow up I want to be an expert.

You will. Whether in soap operas or opera singing, you will be an expert.

For now, the only thing keeping you from realizing your genius is your conflict with yourself. OK, so you can't fly but if someone else can do the thing you admire, then so can you.

Never mind the bollocks.

You're not a baby elephant any more.

At the same time as we're learning lots of simple things, we also need to unlearn our self-imposed restriction of *I can't* – a negative reaction, perhaps caused by trying something that was too difficult before we put in the time, were too young, didn't have the resources or were told by teachers, parents, or worse ourselves, that we were no good at it.

Working toward our objectives involves an incremental series of obstacles, which must be overcome one at a time, moving to other obstacles when we're stuck, but never shelving the stubborn ones until they are resolved one way or another.

*Begin, next, next, next, next, next, next, next, next, next, next, next, next, **Raaargh!!!** Begin again...*

Universal offerings

Whatever our elephant stakes may be, they will dominate our reactions in everything we do until we have pulled them out of the ground and freed ourselves. The clues to locating these stakes aren't very subtle. They are everything that really pisses us off. You know, the stuff we dislike in other people and can't see in ourselves.

This is why we have to be careful with the concept of positive thinking. The danger of trying to think positively all the time is that we can fall into the trap of being motivated into craving for our negative thinking to simply go away.

Flip it round and see what the Universe is offering you. If it's an obstacle, what is the opportunity? Welcome it. Trying to avoid it leaves us yearning for positive thinking, with ever-increasing levels of addiction creating the delusion that something has more plusses than minuses. In the same way, resentment is the delusion that something has more minuses than plusses.

The greater the emotional charge you have for anything, whether through infatuation or resentment, the greater your heart is going to open with gratitude when you discover that the Universe, of which you are part, is perfectly balanced in all things at all times. It is only your **perception of perfection** that needs to catch up.

Later on we're going to make full use of positive thinking, simply by focusing on nothing other than tapping into your inspiration. For now we're simply acknowledging that nothing is difficult. Everything is easy providing we split the parts we think are difficult into small enough and comprehensible increments.

Even if you don't have goals, at one time you did. People give up on goals because they believe the myth of *I can't*. If only there was a button to push, and then we could all live happily ever after...

Ah, we'll come to that.

For now, let's abandon the concept of *I can't* with the courage of the Cheyenne Contraries of the North American plains, who washed in dirt and rode on horseback backwards simply as a means of unlearning. Reframing obstacles as challenges begins the process of pulling stakes from the ground by acknowledging that some of our thought patterns need to be re-rooted.

I'm not going to throw obstacles at you. I'm going to throw beautiful **you** straight back at you, as a means of questioning what you believe is possible. What you believe is possible is your only boundary and, unlike cricket, there's absolutely no way you're ever going to wallop the ball for six beyond it.

So let's make it massive as we gather the hurdle-leaping tools in the upcoming chapters until you open your eyes to the actuality that **your potential is limitless**.

Fuck me, now there's a task.

Well, as it says on the cover of this book, YOUR JOURNEY STARTS HERE.

Let's make a start.

AFFIRMATION
I see all obstacles as opportunities and my momentum is unstoppable.

The Raaargh!!! of Possibilities

When I first met Mike Mckay in my garden, shortly after my family and I moved to Ibiza, he started playing fetch with his dog Chuli. When Chuli started barking, we went to investigate. The ball had fallen into the deep end of a hole, destined to be the swimming pool, and the dog was looking down, still barking, and not fancying the drop. Mike explained to Chuli that all he needed to do was go to the other end where he could walk down easily and get it back, to which Chuli stayed put and barked some more.

What struck me was the sincerity with which Mike spoke to his dog; an oddity too tantalizing for me to let pass without questioning. He told me that he hadn't any idea of how much Chuli could understand, or what was possible, and so he always aimed beyond it, which certainly didn't seem to do him any harm in getting into the *Guinness Book of Records* for creating the world's largest weekly party.

Presuming the fantasy part of our movie to be fact won't get the baby bathed; the real question is whether you would rather be open-minded or close doors within the possibilities of your desires.

There are two aspects to possibilities. The first is the feeling of *I can't* when someone else has already set a benchmark and proved it is humanly possible. The second concerns the limits of human potential in general, while every single day someone somewhere is setting new benchmarks previously believed to be impossible.

So how ambitious was your script and what really are our limits within this great and infinite Universe?

Regardless of whether you break any records yourself *(and why not? I ask you)*, it is wise to expand your understanding while embracing the infinite mystery of our potential, making the acquiring of current benchmarks all the less daunting.

The Raaargh!!! of becoming conscious

The Russian philosopher P.J. Ouspensky said, *'The first stage in realizing human potential is the acceptance that we aren't conscious.'*

Well, if Oupensky was right I'd consider that a fairly significant limitation, but he has a point. To be fully conscious, you need to be completely aware of what is happening **now**, whereas many of our actions and reactions are automatic.

I saw a stunt recently by the excellent Derren Brown, a psychological illusionist, in which he went up to a variety of strangers and asked them for directions. As they spoke he interrupted their flow of well-meaning information by asking them to hold a bottle of water for him. He then asked them to give him their wallet, keys, watch and mobile phone, which virtually all did willingly. As they parted, most realized after a pause that something had happened and went back to him. Amazingly, he offered the things back as if nothing had happened and went over the directions again before repeating the exchange and leaving them walking away without their valuables.

Now, can you see what Ouspensky meant by us not being conscious? We're harping back to the elephant here, and the question still remains: what are we going to do about it? Well, for a start, I seem to remember mentioning something about being grateful for a challenge, but there are really only two choices:

Leave it to chance. In the 1971 novel *The Dice Man* by Luke Rhinehart, the main character realizes he has a number of responses which form a pattern within his life and often don't result in the best outcome. As a solution, every time he has a dilemma he writes out six options, some of which are choices he would absolutely refuse to do usually, and rolls the dice with the certainty he will carry out the option it landed on – an astute observation of the problem, though not the wisest of solutions.

A friend of mine actually tried it out for a few months and ended up living in Italy with a new girlfriend under a false name. An interesting experiment, but needless to say he's not living that way any more.

Surely there must be a better way of finding your inspired destiny than leaving it to the roll of a dice?

Know the answers are inside you. The quality of the answers you receive is dependent on the quality of the questions you ask and, as you are inextricably linked to the entirety of the Universe ...

...the answers are already inside you.

The ultimate search engine is you

Our subconscious mind is limitless and akin to a massive masterpiece, such as Claude Monet's Nympheas (Water Lilies), and the beautiful entirety of that painting is available to us at all times.

Our conscious mind, on the other hand, is only capable of focusing on one piece of pollen on a single flower stem in the background of the painting.

If practical examples are more your thing, then imagine the analogy of a computer. There are many more files and programmes than can be run or opened simultaneously (at the time of writing anyway) and yet we can access everything quite easily. Add the internet to the equation and the amount of information we can access easily is too mind-boggling to comprehend. When you connect a computer to the internet, the full painting of the Nympheas becomes so massive that you would have to step back into outer space to have any chance of seeing it. The whole world is literally at your fingertips.

With intensive training, the human mind is capable of expanding to the point of capacity from perceiving a single piece of pollen to a whole petal of one of those little flowers in the background. With time you can clock up enough experience from different bits of pollen to be able to achieve quite a bit, really.

Wow!

How far you choose to expand this capacity, your thoughts, feelings, memories, knowledge, understanding and wisdom will amount at any one moment in time to a tiny part of the painting.

But how appropriate is the piece of the painting you are likely to choose? In other words, how good is your search engine?

The quality of your search engine is dependent on your level of awareness, and your level of awareness is dependent on how much it is dominated by your automatic reactions, which in turn are proportional to the number of inappropriate labels you have accumulated.

Imagine how life could be if you really did have the ultimate search engine, and you could go into every scenario with the blank canvas of a freshly restarted consciousness.

When you are fully conscious, YOU CAN.

Do you still feel that all your reactions and beliefs in your own limitations are correct and justified?

What do you consider to be a superior mechanism, you or a computer?

Sure a computer can correct your spelling and beat you at chess, but which one is the true miracle?

The Power of Raaargh!!!

Ask yourself the following questions.

Do you think there is significantly more information, understanding and wisdom available to your subconscious RIGHT NOW than you utilize?

YES/NO

Can you see that it is impossible for your brain to process the entirety of that information in one go?

YES/NO

Do you think you have a search engine within your being that is way more inventive than anything currently available on any computer?

YES/NO

Did you know that the only difference between a genius and a normal person is that they live their lives with either a burning curiosity or the intuitive certainty that these three questions were answered YES, which gives them the momentum to keep on searching?

YES/NO

YOU ARE A GENIUS!

YES!

Sheer genius. Yesterday I read about Arran Fernandez, a 15-year-old boy who became the youngest student for more than 200 years to secure a place at Cambridge University. His sole teacher to date has been his father, who said, *'Any child could do this. The idea that babies are born with different amounts of intellectual potential is false. It's fundamentally oligarchic. Home-educated children just find it easier to avoid the dumbing-down process.'*

Yeah, but his dad is a genius, so naturally his kid is too, I hear you say.

So what of the American teacher Marilyn Wilhelm, who consistently gets similar results from the students she teaches, having no entry requirements or streaming process whatsoever and taking on any child with the certainty that they are a genius?

We are all geniuses.

Mind you, the 99 per cent perspiration comes in handy, which is a dream come true if you're doing what you love.

You can either walk around with the perspective of a specific individual piece of pollen, struggling to fit it into context whenever possible, or with the understanding that you have the entirety of the whole painting available to you at all times. Know with absolute certainty that this is true.

And choose.

Life is a series of choices and not making one is a choice in itself.

You can either:

<a> Ignore what I'm saying.

<b> Make this subject the topic for after dinner conversation.

<c> Choose YES!

If you're still not convinced, don't worry, you will be.

Your search engine isn't a question of sourcing particular pieces of data. Google is much better than any human and, if you want to increase your knowledge, according to the champions and trainers, anybody can be trained to speed read or have a photographic memory. The internal search engine I'm talking about works in two ways.

The first is by understanding. This is a far more potent tool than knowledge. Understanding only comes to you when you're ready, so be patient because it generally takes significantly longer than even the internet speed of the old phone modems.

The greatest hindrance to this process is the assumption that opinions are facts. People who believe in a Divine Source, such as God or Buddha, have an advantage in this matter because they humble themselves before an external truth (although people who assume their opinions of the divine to be facts are at a disadvantage). Regardless of what you believe, our conscious minds can't contain the entirety of the Universe as we attempt to catch up with a Universal truth, which not only surrounds us but is also being broadcast via our inner voice, provided we are listening. When something doesn't make sense, have the certainty that the answer will come and work on your ability to wait with an open mind while doing what you can and compromising as you go.

Keep the faith.

The Eighth Principle of Raaargh!!!
The truth is independent of any individual opinions.

Remember this one next time you have a heated argument. If we could see through the eyes of everybody at all times we would be able to see the truth, but as we can't, we must be willing to wait.

Just because it takes us longer to find the answers than Google it doesn't mean that we are not more powerful. The more you think about your specialized subject, which you're doing already, though possibly with resentment, the more reference points you have, which can be triggered by unconnected lateral incidents. Answers come when we are least expecting them, just as the apple fell on Newton's head, or the amber necklace or piece of cake bring the correct diagnosis to Dr House in the US TV show *House*, or the ancient Greek scholar Archimedes shouted '*Eureka!*' in the bath. Although, please note, no lateral *magical* solutions came to any of those people without working toward them in a linear process – waiting while working, being while becoming and having gratitude for challenge – though never punish yourself, as everyone I just mentioned was not without their moments of despair.

Channelling is the second aspect of your search engine. In simple terms, channelling means that the more you focus on the things that inspire you, by putting in the time to train your automatic responses to a chosen skill, the more you tune into allowing creation to happen completely devoid of conscious thought.

A great example is Louis Armstrong's trumpet playing in West End Blues, a composition by Joe 'King' Oliver. You can hear him absolutely pushing the boundaries of harmony. His years of practice and moments of channelling created a quantum leap in terms of music and he changed the sound of jazz and possibilities within it forever (though this is difficult to appreciate unless you ingratiate yourself only with earlier recordings first).

Accessing your search engine is actually easier than it sounds. Just put your faith in the Universe...

So what shall I write about now?

I call upon the mighty powers of the Universe that have never let me down!

Hmm...

Oh!

Raaargh!!!

Perception and reality

So Sir Isaac Newton understood gravity from an apple falling on his head and, while the diagnostic medical team in *House* methodically work through a process of elimination in a linear fashion, Doctor House himself invariably finds the solution from a quantum leap sideways triggered by one of the subplots. If we're to question the limits of possibilities, your movie needs to jump likewise as we cut to a seemingly unrelated scene which will make sense in the fullness of time.

Reality is limited to what can be realized, but what of all the mysterious workings of the Universe beyond our grasp? Perception, reality and actuality are unquestionably not the same thing.

Picasso was asked why his paintings weren't as he saw things in reality, to which he replied that he had no idea what that meant. He was then shown a photograph of the gentleman's wife, to which Picasso replied, *'Ah, so your wife is very small and rather flat.'*

Changing reality; *and it's back to the laboratory.* For many years, scientists have worked on a phenomenon called Random Event Generators (REG). REG machines are able to emulate tossing a coin millions of times using the binary code of 1s and 0s. When you toss a coin, getting it right three times out of three isn't such a big deal, but when you toss a coin a million times, if the number of heads and tails aren't divided equally in a 50/50 split then there's something influencing the experiment.

So REG machines were designed in a way that could faithfully reproduce a completely random set of readings, which always ended up being 50/50 as long as the number of tosses was sufficiently large. These machines were then used to see if just conscious thought alone was sufficiently powerful to influence the results. Normal everyday people, with no claims of being psychic, were asked to have a bash at willing the machine to create more heads than tails through thought alone.

As far as I'm aware, only in the movies can someone look at a chair and instantly make it fly across the room, but on closer inspection the results were nothing short of astonishing and as unlikely as up to a trillion to one of them occurring naturally. The conclusion: yes, conscious beings could influence machines through thought alone.

How exciting to live in an age where science is beginning to recognize the magical properties of thought alone!

Now we really go down the rabbit hole.

I know physics isn't everybody's cup of tea, but please bear with me. Instead of heads or tails, a REG was set up to produce audio clicks, which played randomly in the left or the right ear. When test subjects willed the machine to produce more clicks in one ear than the other, the results matched the results of previous experiments.

Helmut Schmidt then had an inspired idea.

Schmidt had recordings made without witnesses. Nobody ever got to hear the clicks, as there was no one in the room. So were those recordings a set of clicks split equally between left and right?

Who knows?

These recordings were then copied, again without witness. The copy was locked away in a vault and the original recording was played back to a subject to see if they could have any noticeable effect as in the previous experiments.

Again, with odds of a million, a billion and even a trillion to one, they consistently did. Not only was thought alone influencing machine, but also now the recording of something that had already happened was behaving like a machine that was producing these clicks live!

So what's the conclusion to all this?

It wasn't that the tapes were erased and re-recorded, or that history had been altered.

The conclusion was that those recordings were never actually made until they were consciously observed.

If a sunrise isn't witnessed, is it still beautiful? The answer is apparently no, because beauty is a reaction and there's nobody there to react. Well, this experiment seems to be taking it one further and makes you wonder: if nobody is there to witness it, is the sunrise even there?

So what would happen if every conscious being focused upon the same thing?

Is everything possible?

Does the collective '*we*' actually create the world around us as we observe it? And if we all focussed on that chair, could it fly across the room?

Could it be that the Big Bang was an explosion of pure potential consciousness and the Universe is a manifestation of our collective thought as we walk around in each other's dreams?

I don't know.

Embrace the mystery

When the Dalai Lama gave a talk a few years ago at the Albert Hall in London, he gave the same answer to so many questions asked by those gathered including how His Holiness was able to emanate such energy and aura and affect those around him with an overwhelming sense of wellbeing and compassion.

'Hmm... I don't know,' His Holiness chuckled.

It's fascinating that great spiritual people and great scientists are alike in answering so many questions by saying, *'I don't know.'*

Similarly, Socrates, one of the founders of Western philosophy, considered himself to know nothing. After touring round to meet other philosophers professing great knowledge, he decided to his surprise that it was knowledge that hindered them.

Why are you here?

How did you get here?

What are you supposed to do?

Where will we go?

I don't know, but never stop wondering, searching and marvelling at the actuality that you can ask these questions and embrace the mystery of it all.

If you assume you understand things you don't or limit your reality to what you do know, you close the door on the vast majority of what is available to you. All that stuff becomes *I can't.*

You can.

How?

I don't know.

By that I mean that you can do anything someone else has already done and significantly more, providing you don't jump to conclusions. Some elements you don't know yet and others you never will, and yet you will still be able to do it.

The Ninth Principle of Raaargh!!!
Embrace the mystery.
/////////////////////////////////

It's up to you now

You have a choice: ignore the mystery and close your mind or open your mind to the infinite possibilities of the Universe. This choice separates us from animals. If you put 20 dogs in a room, they don't have a choice and war ensues. Ignoring the mystery is tantamount to having the consciousness of a dog.

We exist without knowing how or why, while something amazing is going on under the surface of every part of our lives, which we can't quite put our finger on. As the fundamental root for good living lies in being grateful for existing, I'm all for exaltation and surrendering with dignity to whatever this force may be.

So don't you come quantifying the unquantifiable to me!

Is it more mind-boggling to imagine a whole Universe being created from nothing or that it always has been here?

If in the beginning there was only a creator, what else was there to create anything from other than the creator itself?

Is the divine conscious?

I don't know, but for now let's pause for a moment and be thankful that at least we are, and how many of us there are!

> **'God sleeps in stones, dreams in plants, stirs in animals and awakens in man.'**
>
> **IBN AL-'ARABI**

Universal energy

All energy, matter, beings, ideas, dualities and paradoxes are strands of a universal energy, and are in a constant state of transformation. Right now there are atoms in you which were once in shooting stars. You always have been and you always will be, and the only contentious issue is whether or not your consciousness goes with you.

Is the divine conscious?

I don't know.

But I know that there is no difference between *I* and *we*.

At a subatomic level, the dancer, the other dancers and the dance itself are all one and the same.

The sum of all of our thinking, being and doing is one.

The one is infinite and we are part of it.

Your potential is limitless.

So how far can we take it within this lifetime?

I don't know but, one thing's for certain, there is absolutely no way we can aim beyond what we believe to be possible.

So don't jump to conclusions either about what is or isn't possible while aiming to infinity, and if it isn't possible to pluck all the answers from out there, it's time to take a look within.

AFFIRMATION

I know I am constantly experiencing realms of being beyond my conscious mind through which I can channel my infinite potential.

The Raaargh!!! of Me

Well, this is you movie, which means this is the most important chapter in this book because it is about **your self-esteem: the most powerfully fundamental tool of all!**

Raaargh!!!

The thing is, this whole book is a part of your movie, all of which is aimed at giving you a greater perspective on self-empowerment, making it both easier to achieve and easier for me to write this chapter and therefore feeding two birds with one piece of bread.

I love it when that happens.

There are so many intermingled paths on our journey so, like the chicken and the egg, it's difficult to know which comes first. Being stressed causes your breathing to become shallow and shallow breathing causes you to become stressed. In the same way, self-love generates compassion and compassion generates self-love.

'Do unto others as you would have them do to you.'

JESUS OF NAZARETH

'Consider others as yourself.'

THE BUDDHA

What wonderful words, but before you can incorporate them into your life, consider the wise words of British Airways and all other major airlines, for that matter.

We are told in the safety demonstration, when flying with small children, that in the event of oxygen masks being released we should put on our oxygen masks first before fitting our childrens'. This is due to there being a significant gap between becoming unconscious from a lack of oxygen and dying. Becoming unconscious in an emergency puts the children in our care in far more danger than from losing a few breaths.

Have you heard the one about the difficulties of loving others if you don't love yourself?

Before we help anyone else to put on their masks it is wise to give ourselves some oxygen first, so let's create this motto for ourselves for all times.

The Tenth Principle of Raaargh!!!
Treat yourself as you would like others to treat you.
////////////////

And I mean really treat yourself!

*** EXERCISE 4 ***

Go out and buy flowers for yourself.

Put on your favourite music and dance around the house naked, play the guitar, eat a chocolate bar, read a magazine or cook a wonderful meal.

Have a wank (as Woody Allen said in *Annie Hall, 'Don't knock masturbation! It's sex with someone I love!'*) or have sex with someone you like or love, or just a nap.

Keep up your hobbies because you get to do what you love regardless of any financial payback. Do them while learning to find gratitude for challenge, which can be incorporated in your life as a whole. Do any activity that makes you feel good about yourself.

Take at least one day off a week, or an hour if that's all you've got, and devote the time to you.

Love yourself, look after yourself and, as my wife says, *'If you're depressed, go get depressed on a beach in Brazil.'* Spend time on pursuits, which you enjoy and make you feel good about yourself. This is all about empowering your self-esteem.

Most of us aspire to give our children high self-esteem and if they're pissed off, we do what we can to cheer them up. How would your son or daughter feel if you gave them a really hard time after they'd just had a run-in with the school bully? And yet isn't that what we do to ourselves on a regular basis?

So treat yourself as you would like others to treat you!

Aom

Many people are familiar with the practice of chanting Om, which works like a wave exercise and creates inner bliss. Om is a sacred Hindu symbol which symbolizes Brahman, the omnipresent nature of truth, knowledge and infinity, which is incomprehensible.

A truly balanced Om is Aom.

Aaaaaaaaaa is the sound of self-expression.

Ooooooooooo is the sound of focusing on others.

Mmmmmmmm is the vibration of the balance of unity between yourself (I) and others (we). Your relationship to others and your ability to show compassion are intrinsic to your self-esteem. When the balance is out of kilter, one end of the set of scales drops to the floor, manifesting all manner of problems as they do.

The part of the Universe over which you have most control is you and not caring for yourself won't benefit you or your loved ones, while the Universe will keep on functioning perfectly well regardless. Focusing on others without any *Aaaaaaaaaa* sucks, and focusing on neither fulfils all the requirements of hell.

There are times when we don't feel like connecting with people, and solitude is a most worthy sanctuary. A friend of mine went to Jamaica recently, and how lovely when he was talking loudly to be shushed by a lady pointing out that there was someone sleeping under a nearby tree.

A whispered raaargh...

***EXERCISE 5 ***

Sit cross-legged on the floor or in a chair with your spine as straight as possible and shoulders relaxed.

With your eyes open wide, tilt your head back and begin humming *'Aaaaaaaaaaa'* as a projection of yourself into the infinite Universe.

When you are ready, and without stopping your vocalization, transform the sound to *'Oooooooooooo'*, and lean forward and focus with love and protection, as if toward a small child in a rowing boat in the middle of a choppy lake.

As *'Oooooooooooo'* transforms into *'Mmmmmmmmmmmm'*, straighten your spine and close your eyes, and feel the sound vibrate along the length of your spine and infinitely beyond yourself in both directions.

Breathe in deeply as you open your eyes, leaning back and raising your head to repeat.

Ideally, keep going for at least 20 minutes to see how this powerful incantation can create balance both within you and with the world around you.

Follow the incantation with silence and create a sanctuary within – a blank canvas.

People who struggle with self-expression will struggle more with the *Aaaaa* sound, and people who struggle with focusing on others struggle more with the *Ooooo* sound. This exercise balances both.

The Power of Raaargh!!!

Calm the mind, and everything else falls into place. There is a great technique for when someone is feeling super-stressed. Have them lie on their front and place your hand on their sacrum (the tailbone at the base of the spine), which is comfortable in slightly different positions for different people. Straighten your arms and apply pressure using only your body weight, while listening to the other person to find out how much pressure to apply (the key to all human contact is through listening). This technique moves all excess energy from a busy mind and twitching feet to the centre of the body, and it works.

Hang on, this is about calming other people, whereas this chapter is all about you!

We're back to balancing the scales again; make others feel good and you'll feel good, too. Everything in the Universe exists for good reason, including indulgence in and abstinence from sex, meat, sweets and booze as we endeavour to find balance like a tightrope walker between the spiritual and physical domains, and it sure ain't my job to tell you where to draw the line.

Balancing mind and body

Is it that so many successful/happy people take an interest in their bodies or that taking an interest in your body leads to success and an increased feeling of wellbeing? I don't know, but it often seems to be the way, **though not always**, and I'm reminded of Saint Francis who lived happily in a damp cave, despite arthritis in his knees, or so I'm told.

What I know to be true is that the more work you put into yourself at times when all is well in your life, the greater your arsenal when you're under pressure and stressed. The link between your mind and the Universe is via sensations. It makes sense therefore that our wellbeing, and in turn our success, is dependent upon how we react and what we do with those sensations.

Intellectual thought isn't enough because there is a delicate balance between your heart and mind, as how you feel affects your mental health. Ignoring your body is ignoring how you feel, and this is the main reason we benefit from taking an interest in our bodies.

This book is not about improving your diet and exercise, although there are plenty of superb books on the subject if you think they would be helpful for you. The pointers below are simply to encourage you to focus upon how you feel, which unquestionably will affect the thoughts in your mind.

Your body knows best what to eat. Studies show that diet can make an immense difference to your physical and emotional wellbeing. We are what we eat and all that jazz about food being medicine is absolutely true.

So what should you eat, or even how?

Gandhi said, *'Chew your drink and eat your food,'* meaning take your time, whereas Gudjieff, after living the yogi way, met a wise man in Afghanistan who said yogis don't exercise their stomach muscles, leaving them super weakened in old age, and recommended only semi-chewing rough bones to give the stomach something with which to work.

I'll leave that one with you.

Different diets suit different people and a steak can energize one person and make another person feel sluggish and tired. An expert in macrobiotics told me I drank too much water and was overworking my kidneys. I found out that this was only true for someone who didn't smoke or drink or live in a polluted city and sweat it all out through extreme exercise. I simply dehydrated myself when I didn't drink enough and only drink less water now, as the other factors are no longer relevant.

Listen to your body and respond accordingly. There was a test done on young children in which different food types were laid out for them to choose what they wanted to eat. At first they went for all the junk food, but within a couple of days, free from the constraints of the mind, they picked out a perfectly balanced diet. If you are lacking in potassium, a banana will have greater appeal, but only if you listen to your body. Whether over- or under-eating, listen to your body; it knows.

The influence of diet on the balance between body and spirit is huge. The mind can play such an important role, especially if diets create a sense of sacrifice or guilt.

Imagine a group of people not eating any food for several days: one is fasting on a spiritual quest to explore the nature of attachment; another wants to lose weight; the third is anorexic and underweight; another on a detox; the next is too sick to eat; the sixth is on a political hunger strike; and then there's the poor bloke who simply can't get his hands on any food.

Each of them is doing exactly the same thing and yet they have different intentions. I find fasting the most powerful tool of them all, though I won't go further as it's all a question of intention.

Your '*why*' changes everything. Let me tell you that the best laid intention to focus on diet and exercise, other than your body being your temple or the vehicle for your soul, is because the only obstacle to generating self-love are your thoughts alone.

That's it.

The link between your consciousness and the Universe is via sensations. The greatest priority to generate self-love is listening to those sensations.

We've looked at acquiring answers from looking outwardly, whereas this chapter is about looking within. Not listening to your body, just like ignoring your inner voice, makes those answers and guidance a greater hindrance. It is only when we listen to the feelings and sensations, which are happening **now.** When you are present, you can gain great pleasure by simply walking barefoot on the grass or by feeling the wind running through your hair, just as the wind is having a right old blast too.

In the meantime, if you want an ice cream, have one because that's a good sensation, too. The balance between the physical and spiritual domains is affected by time and the benefits and drawbacks in the short and long term. Just understand that addictions are the illusion that there are more benefits than drawbacks to a particular thing, while there is no *good* or *bad* in anything.

George Gurdjieff, an extraordinary spiritual teacher, wrote of many of his greatest lessons from all of his greatest teachers in *Meeting with Remarkable Men*. He said that the lesson of greatest benefit to him was his father's way of putting insects and mice in his bed and waking him up every morning by throwing a cold bucket of water over him, regardless of the weather, and making him run around naked.

Raaargh!!!

Now, I'm not suggesting you do this and adopt an *I'm a Celebrity Get Me Out of Here!* approach, which is an awful way of dealing with phobias. It is, however, worth noting that Gurdjieff said it was this practice that enabled him not to react to hardships and treat them simply as events which needed to be sorted out. The calmer the mind to avoid unnecessary reactions and the better equipped your body is physically, the less you will react negatively to any challenges thrown at you.

Your body, your choice. Being physically fit has many obvious health benefits, all of which are helpful in creating high self-esteem, too. For example, exercise reduces cortisol, a stress hormone which causes problems such as weight gain and reduced sex drive. Exercising releases a number of chemicals, including serotonin and dopamine, which can improve your mood and put you more in touch with your needs.

As I said earlier, this isn't a diet and exercise book, but getting off your backside and avoiding stagnation is a must, and the joy of using your body can be the greatest meditation of them all.

The type of exercise you choose is up to you, but the following aspects of physical health are particularly helpful for your wellbeing and self-esteem.

- When participating in hard exercise, or the next time you lift something heavy, concentrate on relaxing the face. Pain in the body (which some trainers will tell you is *the weakness coming out!)* needn't be expressed in the face. This is a very powerful way of learning to separate discomfort from reaction.

- Learn to relax your neck and shoulders while exercising the legs and abdomen, as tension there goes hand in hand with tension in the mind.

- Deep abdominal breathing, as taught in yoga and martial arts, is intrinsic to meditation to help you overcome stress, and focusing on your breath immediately puts you into the present.

- Get in touch with the centre of your body located between your pubic bone and navel. All action and your ***Raaargh!!!*** are created here.

- Work on your posture and having a straight spine because at times when you feel utterly helpless, standing tall makes everything seem conquerable, and throw in a quick ***Raaargh!!!*** by all means.

Your body is your temple, but don't get too obsessed with diet and exercise because the effects of obsession won't help you quieten the mind either.

Forgetting to be

Every benefit has a drawback just as every drawback has a benefit. Being obsessed with improving yourself all the time can mean you start being self-critical and giving yourself a hard time. Feelings of failure and guilt, just like resentment, lead to stagnation and not focusing on either **being** or **becoming**. Even if we're progressing toward our goal two steps forward and one step back, those backward steps will inevitably lead to us forgetting our progress and filled to the brim with self-loathing.

Aaargh!!!

The less you punish yourself for feeling like an arsehole, the quicker understanding will come for whatever it is you need to incorporate into your life with gratitude. Don't worry about it. Being an arsehole is necessary on occasions. Just know with certainty that everything will be absolutely fine.

Despite the fact that any crap we happen to be experiencing will serve as a fertilizer for our next harvest of manifestations, it certainly doesn't feel that way at the time. If you've messed up, great! So what now? Just move on, quieten the mind and remove any label as quickly as possible, and be patient for the coming of new understanding.

Creation comes from nothing and everything's going to be just fine because, regardless of whether anything happens for a reason, love is your reality and new creation and inspiration will arise out of anything, provided you allow them to.

The 11th Principle of Raaargh!!!
There is no such thing as a mistake.

///

Letting go and finding joy

You are wonderful and innocent, a cherished miracle of the Universe with all of time eternal to get it right through a series of actions born from letting go, which culminate with the realization you need do nothing.

When you surrender and accept yourself just the way you are, this will be your ultimate moment.

Sometimes we do what we have to, or ought to, or need to, or want to, or desire to, or choose to, but today (or pencil a date in) just do what you love to do.

I like to take the dogs for a walk. From a purely self-indulgent point of view, the natural feeling of joy they express provokes joyfulness in me. In the same way that a group of people laughing at nothing much in particular can lead to genuine prolonged hysterics, I find it quite difficult to be grumpy around a dog's wagging tail. Add the infectious wave-form tranquillity of nature and you've got yourself a winner.

This is because the natural world conveys waves of feeling, too. Have you ever wondered why staring out of the window makes you feel better or why babies stop crying if they're taken into the garden? The straight architectural lines of interiors combined with clutter represent human particle thought, while nature's lines remain transient and wavelike. We are drawn to beaches and mountains because they calm the mind and allow us to simply **be** in the environment, away from the busyness of life.

Hobbies are intrinsic to achieving our dreams. They are something we choose to do and there's no reason why your hobby can't become your dream job.

At a time when Marcela and I were struggling to maintain a harmonious marriage *(a marriage without obstacles offers few gains),* I would pick up my guitar and fill my being with the idea that *nothing's gonna change my world.* I wrote two albums of love songs which turned out to the greatest affirmation of life and love imaginable (not to be confused with challenge-free!)!

The Power of Raaargh!!!

There's this tendency for love songs to be pure fantasy, based on wanting to live happily ever after and creating a massive delusion for unwary up-and-coming teenagers. My love songs worked more along the lines of...

Even though you make the rules,

Even though you break my balls,

I know I'll always be with you.

At times I didn't know how the situation would resolve itself, but the answers came as they always do, though only when I was ready for them.

Writing love songs gave me the time and space I needed. Trying to sort things out with a busy mind is counterproductive and it's important to know when to give yourself a break. So many times I've had an impossible deadline and found myself staring at the computer for hours and then simply gone to bed and woken up with a fresh head and finished everything off rapidly with a refreshed mind.

Ah, but if only I had the time for breaks, now!

S.N. Goenka, the head of Vipassanā Meditation talked at length about creating time. He headed a department of the civil service in Burma, as he was renowned both for his honesty and efficiency. He still found time to meditate every morning and evening, and was so incredibly efficient that he ended up heading five different government departments.

The more time you dedicate to whatever calms your mind, the greater your focus will be when it's time to act. It's great to try new things, too, to broaden your possibilities and increase your sense of adventure. Marcela tried snorkelling for the first time this summer, and her obvious hysterical delight was as gratifying for her as for anybody witnessing the event. It took a few goes before she could keep her head under for more than a couple of seconds because she kept surfacing with the hysterical cry of *'Flipando!'*

There are always new things you can try, and the vast majority are within your budget because the coolest stuff comes free.

The Raaargh!!! of meditation

So now we come to the Ferrari of everything that is *The Power of Raaargh!!!* Meditation practice unquestionably creates the ultimate longer lasting blank canvas while removing all labels and addictions in the process.

The meditation I practise is called Vipassanā. I'm not saying it's the best, as I have no way of knowing, though I have never spoken to any practitioner who knows of a better system, and it is unquestionably perfect.

To fully appreciate this practice of focusing on your sensations you have to practise it for ten days, and no one who hasn't completed the full ten days can either pay for it or partake in shorter sittings. (You don't pay but leave a donation to allow others to practise with the gratitude that you were paid for by someone else.) Now this sounds kind of tough, and I guess in one way it kind of is, and many people don't finish the course.

I heard it described recently as the way of the hero or heroine, which will attract some people while putting others off. For my part I disagree, as everything is about breaking it down into lots of little things. There are two aspects to meditation – awareness and equanimity (viewing everything without bias – *bliss, pain, subtle, strong*).

There is no question that anyone starting to practise meditation will have a busy mind and discomfort when sitting still for prolonged periods. Like everything, it's a question of tension and release, and treating both with equanimity. Push yourself as hard as you possibly can and go '*fuck it*' by taking time for the odd rerun of your favourite TV show should it crop up. Release creates the blank canvas for new tension, and a life without both is crap.

Just as **Raaargh!!!** can be a nano-meditation, combining both tension and release simultaneously, the more you practise mediation for prolonged periods, the greater you will incorporate a finely tuned balance of tension and release within your life. Although it's worth remembering that balance is already happening – it's just that our reactions to *Aaargh!!!* can drag on a bit.

During the ten days you don't speak and afterwards I couldn't believe how deeply I'd gone simply by focusing on sensations, despite all the distractions. On the last day, I stood up and went outside and stood side on to another guy. After a brief pause I turned my head and made eye contact.

BOOM!!!

It was like being reborn and looking straight into my mother's eyes, not that I can remember, but it was like seeing everything for the first time again.

I've found it!

Bollocks you have!

The full ten days create the ultimate reference point and now I can return to that place with great effect (and varying levels of awareness) very quickly. So, like many things in this book, I'm just sowing a seed. Just know that it is there should it ever take your fancy.

But any time spent in solitude and being present creates awareness and equanimity. A tightrope walker can have awareness without equanimity and a stone can be without bias while being utterly unaware (at least not in a time frame we can comprehend). Meditation allows you to focus with impartiality on the bliss in the forehead, the pain in the knees and the subtlest sensations in the body – perhaps in the left forearm.

This is true equanimity and what a tool to take out into the world around us. Not only does meditation enable efficiency by creating a blank canvas in your mind, but it also fills your sensations with love and compassion. Equanimity brings choice because you are fully present in the moment. In the event someone shouts at you, instead of simply reacting by shouting back, you differentiate between why they are shouting at you, the fact they are shouting at you, whether or not you can do anything about it (and thereby do it), or whether there is nothing you can do. Simply not reacting usually placates the other person and provokes discussion rather than an argument.

There is no question that anybody starting to practise meditation will have a busy mind. With practice and focus on sensations there will become points of great bliss in the mind, though take it in your stride.

Calm the mind and everything will fall into place.

The Raaargh!!! of liberation

So am I physically fit, a healthy eater and meditate?

Well, no; I'm less fit than I've ever been, eat well when my body tells me (I'm certainly not adverse to eating crap) and meditate when it is helpful.

Diet, exercise and meditation, however, have been essential over the years for rebalancing myself when I was overwhelmed with the power of *Aaargh!!!*

Some years ago, I suffered a spell of mental illness after taking a malaria pill called Larium. Although, it took me six years to find out I hadn't actually had a nervous breakdown and didn't really need to jack in my job in the movies and explore the world of parties, music and flying trapeze.

But what flowers grew from that shit!

I now know enough to know that all these techniques generate self-love and compassion from *The Power of Aaargh!!!* phenomenally quickly and with absolute certainty.

Raaargh!!!

The same certainty I had for writing the best possible book in the available time I will now place in working on my health, which I've neglected in order to meet my deadline.

So, why is it so important to me that I reveal my weaknesses in this book?

It's because they are not weaknesses, as the power of *Aaargh!!!* is a wonderful tool of learning. I'm not suggesting you adopt any self-depreciating proclamations; it all depends on where you're coming from.

It has never occurred to me that I wasn't both a genius and an arsehole, as both these states are completely normal for everybody. Extra**ordinary** is a word that describes merely our stunned reactions to things which are perfectly normal regardless of whether or not we're used to them.

I have been described as a genius here and there over the years.

Bighead!

Well, yes and no.

I'm as open about my genius as about being an arsehole because **we are all** both.

There are numerous definitions of genius, the one that I find most relevant being: **the ability to channel such skills into productive outlets**.

So in that regard, anybody who doubts we are all geniuses has a point, but anyone can channel the skills which inspire them into productive endeavours. In this aspect, **you are** unquestionably a *potential genius*. Fulfil that prophecy now as:

'To understand the heart and mind of a person, look not at what he has already achieved, but at what he aspires to.'

KAHLIL GIBRAN

Allow your genius to realize that the *Power of Aaargh!!!* is highlighting areas in your life which need attention and never doubting doubt. It is a lie that comes as a friend if only you can wait till you discover its hidden meaning.

So now we go full circle in this chapter as I talk again of self-esteem and let me pump you up with the affirmation that **you are an arsehole!**

It's liberating!

It is only through the embracing of this divine wonderment of dualities that you are able to harness the powers of *Aaargh!!!* and *Raaargh!!!* and thus discover how to channel your genius.

The early stages involve separating the wheat from the chaff and, with time, the proportion of your harvest will shift to an opposite bias as you enjoy the process of working toward almost chaff-free wheat.

This process is only possible by channelling our recognized genius while being grateful for the arsehole within us to guide us when we have wandered off the path.

Only by accepting this actuality can you generate an ongoing and liberating self-esteem.

Isaac Newton gets my vote as being the most fulfilled intellectual genius of all time. He was useless at school, constantly dreaming, socially inept and it was his inventions, rather than his limited mathematics, which made his uncle enrol him into Cambridge. In Newton's second year, his professor resigned in recognition that Isaac was superior in his understanding of mathematics.

Nobody consistently made as many astounding breakthroughs, discoveries and inventions as Newton.

One of them was the cat flap.

He was tired of the cats opening his door, flooding the room with light and interfering with his experiments, so he cut a small door just for them.

What a genius!

When his cat had kittens, he had the inspired idea of cutting a smaller door next to the bigger door for the kittens to go through.

What an arsehole!

So that's it; take the rest of the day off and go and do whatever you want.

And if you fear loneliness, run toward it on occasion, because there is no company more rewarding than your own.

AFFIRMATION
I love myself as I am, creating freedom within my vulnerability and honouring myself to further empower my ideal self.

Raaargh!!! Can Mean Anything and that Includes No!

In 1966, John Lennon climbed the stepladder at the art exhibition at the Indica Gallery in London to see what was written in tiny letters on the ceiling. The writing was so small he needed a magnifying glass, which as luck would have it was hanging from a piece of string.

Looking through the magnifying glass he read *'YES!'*

What a word! Inspired, he sought out the artist Yoko Ono and, as they say, the rest is history. We all love hearing the word **yes**, the treasure of an answer we all seek.

'Can I have an ice cream and will you sleep with me?'

The sweet reply of *'yes'* is a manifestation in itself.

Another word associated with manifestation is *'producing'*. Everyone's contribution in the collaborative art of moviemaking is essential but if there's one role responsible for the fact the film exists, it's the producer.

And yet there's another reply we're more likely to get from them than anyone else.

'No!'

'Can we shoot in the North Pole?'

'No.'

'Well, how about an extra £5 million?'

'No.'

'So I suppose an extension on our shoot dates is out of the question?'

'Yes.'

We can ask anybody for anything we want, which works to our benefit providing we respect the reply of *'no'*. What goes with this idea is the necessity to embrace our ability to reply to the humble requests and intrusions from other people, too. Your movie is your movie and the production of your manifestations is the responsibility of you alone. To make a great movie of your choosing, you must make decisions as you go.

Guide your projects by being a master at both *'yes'* and *'no'*.

How often do people feel they can only say *'no'* with anger? And, if you remember, if you can't manage your emotions, you can't manage anything. You can avoid this situation by mastering the most powerful magic word in the Universe for warding off resentment: **'NO'**.

Raaargh!!!

I often chat philosophy with my eldest son, who asked me the other day whether my book was about how not to be a bastard while not being a mug. I had to think... *surely there was more to it than that*... but after a brief hesitation I figured he was right and suggested he get a job in marketing.

Loving yourself requires keeping it that way and opening your heart to loving the world around you but in so doing, you leave a wide-open gap for the wolves to steam in.

In the same way that getting burned emotionally leads to the conclusion *no one's ever going to do that to me again,* locking the door and throwing away the key, we need to draw the line somewhere, so let's draw the line out of choice.

The solution to this conundrum lies in understanding the difference between a barrier and a boundary. A barrier is an impregnable wall, which restricts the flow of movement in both directions. No one and nothing, including opportunities, can get in and you can't get out.

I won't ever trust a man again is a conclusion which will lead to exactly that outcome. If you have these types of feelings, Exercise 2 as well as Vipassanā Meditation, among many other paths, are great at dissolving these labels; both evolve our understanding that labels and opinions are not the same thing as facts.

A boundary on the other hand is transient; its limits are constantly evolving, with you being responsible for drawing the line.

A boundary has a door that neither needs to be left wide open nor locked securely, for it has a bouncer standing at the entrance, and that bouncer is YOU!

The management reserve the right of entry; whether he or she is a known troublemaker, wearing the wrong shoes or you're going with your gut instinct.

YOU'RE NOT COMING IN!

Who's in charge, anyway?

So this chapter is about creating and knowing your boundaries, smack bang in between the chapter on self-love and the love of others. Where else was it going to go?

Children are crying out for boundaries and saying *'no'* is an act of love, which is demonstrated by children who grow up unfamiliar with the concept. Intuitively children know it's not appropriate to be in charge just yet and play up through a need to understand their limits. It's their job to push boundaries as they evolve up the hierarchy from dependant to contributor. It's the job of the parent and teacher to say *'no'*, which is why hierarchy is not a bad thing and is a form of collective love.

Hierarchy has nothing whatsoever to do with being inferior or superior to anybody, and neither is it better or worse. Wherever you're at in the pecking order, it's perfect. Just keep growing with evolutionary momentum like the first fish that crawled from the sea and if you do it with gratitude for challenge, it'll feel perfect too.

Dogs, for example, are pack animals and become confused when they don't know their position in the hierarchy. When human owners let their dog be in charge in certain situations, it confuses them and gives a mixed message. The point being, a dog is happy regardless of whether they are at the top or the bottom of the pecking order, providing they know their position. Dog owners, or rather dog guardians, bless 'em, need to let them know who's in charge.

Lion taming is not the most lovingly constructive use of human understanding, but nevertheless, the following example sheds light into the workings of hierarchy.

If you watch a lion tamer in action, you'll notice he always goes into the cage before the lions. This means the lions are coming into his territory because entering a lion's territory is a great way to get eaten. Interestingly the star of the show is the lion at the bottom of the hierarchy and the top lion is the one that does the least – *don't ask too much of him*. In the wild, there is only one adult male in a pride, though in a pack of dogs there are many and, if it wasn't for hierarchy, they'd all be constantly fighting; sorting out every single little clash of interest with violence, resulting in the weakest coming out worse off, so hierarchy works with love for them too.

This is also true of raising children. The greater part of our self-discipline as adults arises from the discipline (meaning to teach) we received as children. My old school housemaster, Ralf Dunning, who taught Latin and terrified kids with his roar *'YOU BOY!'*, was was also one of the ones who cared the most. At 11, I went through a phase of being disillusioned by school and boy did I get it. He took such disciplined action that I went from bottom to top of the class within a few months. Since that time, I have held him in high esteem with gratitude, love and affection, and was saddened that I never got to thank him before he died. But he knew.

Thank you Ralf Dunning and I'm crying again. Tears are the way of the warrior, and this is as good as it gets.

Knowing when to say 'yes'

It all goes wrong when a parent, teacher or guardian doesn't know when to allow the child some independence, and it is equally essential to master when to say 'yes'. Taditionally, the Japanese were among the strictest of cultures and Masahiro Oki, Japan's most advanced yogi who combined yoga with Zen Buddhism, never dared question his father when he said *'no'*. But his father also knew when to say *'yes'*. When Oki asked his dad if he could jump off the roof of the house, his father piled all the mattresses one on top of the other in the garden, and off Oki jumped.

Knowing when to say *'yes'* and *'no'* is an essential skill and a constant work in progress as we rise in the hierarchy and gain responsibility. Many of our abilities stem from how good our parents were at teaching us. There is no question they were always acting for our interests with the utmost love to the maximum capacity of their understanding, interpreted in turn with our own capacity, which is why at times it certainly didn't **seem** that way.

The fewer boundaries our parents instilled, the less likely we are to respect other peoples' and the more intrusive they were, the less likely we are to respect our own boundaries.

Either way, it doesn't matter. Parents make mistakes and pass them down to their children who, quite possibly, pass the opposite characteristics to their children as a way of balancing things out.

Nevertheless the effect is same, like a car pile-up on the motorway, because sooner or later one of the drivers is going to apply the brakes in time, and all the easier if you have gratitude for your ancestors, you want that driver to be you. If you had parents who didn't understand boundaries, you still have the power to control your life by empowering yourself with self-love and compassion while mastering the ability to say *'no'*.

Whether the boundary refers to you, your territory, or those under you care, you are the doorman (or woman), so let's begin with how to be a 'firm but fair' bouncer.

The 12th Principle of Raaargh!!!
Know whose territory this is and that you have absolute authority.
//

Raaargh!!!

Defending your boundaries

Inspired and in need of research, I signed up for a course, and this inspirational author is also a licensed doorman. The course was tremendously insightful – and entertaining too – especially when a large man with a shaved head and sunglasses asked toward the end of the course when it was time to do the weapons training. The only weapon you need is **no means NO.**

Other than all the useful information on fire extinguishers and the like, the most relevant pieces of information for protecting your own boundaries are below.

Know the terms of the entrance policy. In terms of your body, this is none of my business. When it comes to your external boundaries, it becomes significantly more complicated than meeting the criteria for getting into the nightclub.

If you know your priorities then great, which is why a mission statement makes things so much more efficient. If it's a grey area, don't feel obliged to answer right away unless you absolutely have to.

Listen. Explain. Be open for feedback and have a think if you need to. When you make a decision stick to it until new developments bring the need for further consideration. If my children can logically explain why it's best to do otherwise, then they are rewarded with a *'yes'*.

Otherwise, know that no means no and never back down. If you need to discuss it, stand so that they are facing the way out, not the way in. Once you've made your decision, stick to it. If ignored, presume they didn't understand and go over your reasons again. Be open for more feedback but make sure they know your final decision.

Next time get heavy and if they try it again, tell them to go forth and follow their own priorities. With good communication, this rarely happens. When it comes to my kids, I say in a calm voice and maintaining eye contact that I'm willing to take this all the way, and it ends there because they know I will. But *Raaargh!!!* they take the piss the rest of the time, which is fine with me.

Maintain eye contact. Well, there you go. As an equal among equals, I can't stress enough the importance of having good eye contact. (Exercise 9 can help you become more comfortable with eye contact.) Whether you're an employer or employee, be comfortable looking anybody in the eyes.

Don't maintain eye contact if they pull a gun on you; face your palms toward them and look at the space in the middle between your chest line. Well, hopefully that one won't be necessary, but it's important to realize not to make eye contact with everyone, particularly if you are walking through a dodgy area or got a bootful of stolen trophies.

If in doubt, fake it!

There was a wonderful series on the BBC called *Faking It*. Each episode involved taking the least likely candidate possible for a particular skill, training them up for a few weeks or so by the best trainers available and then presenting them to a panel of experts who had to work out which one was faking it.

My favourite episode was the one when a rather small, meek and mild man was chosen to train as a nightclub bouncer. He was phenomenal! Competing with a group of muscle-bound professionals, none of the specialist panel thought for a moment that this man hadn't been a hardened doorman *(as they prefer to be called)* for years.

Anyone can do it. And that includes you. The only way to be charming, open-hearted and filled with self-respect and respect of others is by using the word *thank you,* and the self-assurance that comes with the certainty that *no* means *no.* Stand back in awe of how you receive more, not less respect when you say *'no'.* Saying *'no'* is also sexy, as women know to their advantage, because playing hard to get makes us guys go crazy and makes the *'yes'* ever more gratifying. Fortunately, *Sex and the City* was beneficial in redressing this balance, and saying *'yes'* immediately is absolutely fine too!

Everything becomes a choice once you become a master at saying no, because everything you do from this point is out of choice, taking action out of love and inspiration.

You cannot be a master of self-expression unless you are a master at saying *'no'.*

Just say *'no'* to absolutely anything you choose and, unless you want to, don't feel obliged to justify your decision. If you don't say *'no'*, who is really the cause of your resentment? The liberty taker who asked?

No, your resentment is your responsibility and lies, while the *'liberty taker'* is a negative label you've given to the unconscious loving act of another, who is presenting you with a well needed opportunity for self-empowerment.

The Raaargh!!! of 'no' in action

My wife took a very powerful man out to lunch to ease some communication problems between him and a client. Their first exchange of words went as follows. He ignored my wife and told his sparkly girlfriend to go and get the car, throwing the keys in her general direction. With the speed and grace of a ninja, Marcela reached out and caught them, instantly throwing them back at him adding, *'We've both got heels on. You get it.'*

They've been the closest of friends ever since.

Being comfortable saying *'no'*, together with eye contact, brings with it increasing levels of self-assurance to throw the ball back when challenged. There are many times in life when we are outside our territory and people will still try it on.

If you're not remotely bothered, great! But if you find yourself thinking about it later, be grateful for the lesson to empower yourself at throwing the ball back rather than punish yourself or seek revenge.

Q: 'Wow, love the look of your book The Power of Raaargh!!! Can I borrow it?'

A: 'I want to read it again and nobody ever gives anything I lend back, but I thoroughly recommend buying your own copy - it's available in all good online and high street bookshops.'

Alternatively just say,

'No!'

No comes in many forms. I was at a noodle bar with my younger son recently, where the lady behind the counter asked him whether he was a boy or a girl. Well, I can't see that one going down well with any child, and I *Raaarghed!!!* internally as he replied, 'Are you Chinese or Japanese?'

Sure, we don't want to go through life disregarding the uniqueness of different Oriental cultures, but there are no real rules to life as we learn and, let's face it, she had it coming, and it was love in the form of challenge for them both.

In the book *Little Big Man* by Thomas Berger (way better than the film), as Custer was massacring an Indian village, the chief told his son it simply wasn't a good day to die and told him they'd avoid death by becoming invisible. They walked through the massacre and nobody touched them. Perhaps they were invisible or, perhaps, they just looked like they belonged and were assumed to be Indian scouts working for the army but, either way, they were ignored. Gurdjieff tells a similar story when leading a large group of students through territories of both sides of the Russian Revolution without even being questioned once.

Fear attracts problems

Even on a national level, dictators can only seize power of a country gripped with fear. So look at your fears as being indicators of areas which you need to empower.

Walk around with a feeling of protection, like the glow in the old Ready Brek cereal commercials, and see how everybody leaves you alone. Any martial arts master will tell you they never get into fights because they resonate self-assurance and people don't try it on. Self-assurance means you don't need to fight, so as that is the case, you don't need to bother.

I'm a massive fan of the Barefoot Doctor's *School for Warriors* classes, which you can download from his website (www.barefootdoctorglobal.com). He picks eight areas of personal power from the martial arts and it is the best system I know for incorporating these principles into your life without 20 years of knuckle press-ups.

Another technique, of course, is to simply shout **Raaargh!!!** as often as possible.

On the other hand, those 20 years of knuckle press-ups is no *bad* thing, and being super tasty and up for it – if the cause is great enough (which for the numerous cases I've witnessed it never was) – eliminates the very fear which causes all those unnecessary incidents.

So while Mahatma Gandhi said,

'Victory attained by violence is tantamount to a defeat, for it is momentary.'

He also said,

'Violence is any day preferable to impotence. There is hope for a violent man to become non-violent. There is no such hope for the impotent.'

And I'd like to thank *The A-Team* remake for turning me on to both quotes.

So let me end this chapter with another story about Masahiro Oki, which shows what can be achieved when you understand both boundaries and compassion.

One time a disturbed man came to his dojo, where he taught, and said that he'd always wanted to kill a great man and had come to kill him. So Oki let him in and put the kettle on. He explained to the man that as he was super hard and as the other had no gun, he had no chance whatsoever of achieving his goal.

As Oki taught people to proceed toward their goals, he then proceeded to teach his assailant how to kill him.

He taught him how to use a knife, how to walk silently so he didn't wake him and how to climb over the roof, and to enter Oki's room via the back door, which was always unlocked.

It was at this point that Oki admitted to feeling a little afraid. After three days, when the man still hadn't killed him, Oki approached him and asked why. The man replied that he now admired Oki so much that he no longer wished to kill him.

Oki scolded and beat him furiously with a stick asking him what kind of a man he was not to stick to his goals, and wrote, *'After that he changed very much.'*

AFFIRMATION

I am the driver of my own life and everywhere I go is of my own choosing.

The Raaargh!!! of We

Art imitates life and many a movie is filled with arguments. I'm sure yours is, too, and so the aim of this chapter is to turn conflict into compassion, which is a work in progress for all of us.

When a dispute arises, at first we feel that it is 100 per cent the other person's fault, as they think likewise of us. With time and experience we become big enough to admit to ourselves that the blame lies equally in a 50/50 split.

Both scenarios are illusions because the world is a mirror.

Your problems are 100 per cent your responsibility and other people's problems are 100 per cent theirs.

Every criticism you shout at anyone else is about yourself. Although it may have been triggered by other people's actions, you are so busy listening to negative emotions that you fail to see the trait in yourself.

Of course your criticism is true of them, too, though they will see it out of context and time, while the

Universe has thrown you together as an opportunity for shared self-learning. You'll know this is true because most of us find it hard to contain our indifference to people who don't expose our shortcomings.

Provided this wisdom is received with gratitude rather than self-deprecation, you're onto a winner.

I wrote earlier that the *Principles of Raaargh!!!* are about acquiring the balls or ovaries of a train robber with the loving desire to be fair. Well, here it is. Tolerance and kindness create harmonious and constructive relationships, which in return empower your ability to be assertive. Pretty soon you'll find that the people around will start to mirror your behaviour and find ways to be more tolerant and kinder to you. In the meantime, be grateful for the irritations caused by others and treat them as challenges to be overcome.

Part of the transformation from *Aaargh!!!* to *Raaargh!!!* is the alleviation of fear, because when you look for the good in other people, you generate interaction with their positive aspects and automatically have less to fear.

'I'm selfish, impatient and a little insecure. I make mistakes, I am out of control and at times hard to handle. But if you can't handle me at my worst, then you sure as hell don't deserve me at my best.'

MARILYN MONROE

Meetings and greetings

In the meantime I'll ease off the gas and tell you why I started using the word *Raaargh!!!* and how it is instrumental in influencing your relationships with other people to everyone's benefit.

Raaargh!!!

Different cultures have evolved different ways of greeting people: a bow, a discussion about the weather or the spring blossoms in one culture, offering a herbal tea or aiming a bow and arrow at each other's chests in another.

Ignoring these protocols and steaming straight into, *'Oy Paddy, where's the bog?'* is a great way of walking into trouble.

Fortunately for the disrespectful Englishman in this encounter in Dublin, Paddy *(yes, he'd actually got his name right)* was a master of the power of *Raaargh!!!* A general hush fell across the bar, as Paddy, who had a formidable reputation in those parts, replied to the giddy glee of those gathered, *'Go to the end of the bar, turn right, go straight ahead and you'll come to a door with a sign on it that says "Gentlemen". Don't mind that... just go on in.'*

In a nutshell, when greeting those we don't know, our first priority is determining whether the other person is friend or foe.

With the current world population at over 6 billion people, most of us have simply stopped asking. Instead we ignore strangers and save our greetings for the people we meet, most of whom we already know and, depending on where we live, we offer a handshake, a kiss on the cheek (in Spain two, in Holland three), a nose rub or a hug.

Many people start a conversation with *'How are you?'* to which in Argentina they reply, *'Well or shall I tell you?'*

What the Argentines realize is that the reason we ask has nothing to do with wanting to find out. Have you ever noticed someone reply, *'I'm fine... fine, how are you?'* and maybe even repeat it when you hadn't even asked in the first place?

The real reason we go through these social protocols is because we're stalling for time. This is because it takes us a few seconds to adjust to whom we're talking to and remind ourselves what role we need to play. We like to think we're one unified individual and yet adopt completely different personas when talking to our mum, a policeman, the vicar, a child, the boss, the person we fancy, our partners and so on; we continually create new personas in response to new events or people.

Writing this book, for example, has challenged me to find my writer's voice – the universal me. Hmm...

We learn to identify with a host of different *I*s, not to mention a dazzling array of *them.* Encounters demand that we pause to take stock of the scenario before choosing and uploading the required role for the job. Needless to say, we are not living consciously, as we rely on familiar and automatic patterns, thus postponing living in the here and now.

So how are you?

Which I will you choose?

And for that matter, what is I?

Setting the tone

The quality of these roles we create for ourselves determines whether a room lights up when we enter or leave it, as well as the quality of the whole series of movies in which we find ourselves living.

Have you ever noticed the phenomenon of how often people reply to *'How are you?'* or *'Are you well?'*, with the meek but optimistic reply of *'Oh, not bad.'*

This reply is attempting to be positive through expressing a double negative, while unwittingly taking *'badness'* for granted as being the state of normality.

We can do better than that.

One friend of mine, whose father used to tell him, *'Son, aim low and you won't be disappointed,'* would call me up and start with the line, *'It's only me.'*

Only me?

YOU'RE A LIVING GOD, MAN!

The way you start a conversation sets the tone for how it will continue and most opportunities will be born from these humble beginnings. Greetings are the foundation for many a manifestation. Robert Watts, the producer of *Star Wars*, told me that his success was partly due to the fact that he could remember the name of virtually everybody he'd ever met.

So saying *'Oh not bad,'* is not a great vision of where you want to go. In a best case scenario things won't turn out too bad and, although you don't want to be let down, you are already focusing on the possibility, which makes it the most likely outcome.

'Oh, not bad, thanks,' often leads to a good old moan about the price of bread and, as they say, a problem shared is a problem doubled. The part you never got to hear was how that person was looking for someone to

embark upon a quest which just so happened to be your ideal destiny.

Now, sometimes we do feel bad. Sometimes we need a shoulder to cry on and are wise to have a carefully selected confidant or two. But taking badness for granted as the norm and blabbering it out to all and sundry is the most powerful technique for feeling like crap for as long and as often as you possibly can. This is why Ouspensky stressed that we should avoid voicing negative emotions. Feeling them is one thing, but moaning creates neural pathways in the brain which label the world as unfair. Given enough nourishment, these pathways grow fatter and fatter, making your reactions *seem* more and more justified.

Aaargh!!! becomes your reality.

Aaargh!!! to Raaargh!!!

I noticed this social phenomenon about myself at a time in my life when I was struggling emotionally, while simultaneously producing huge stage shows in the name of fun in the fickle club world in Ibiza. Replying *'Oh not bad,'* simply wouldn't do.

After all, I was feeling bad at the time.

So I replied, *'Amazing!'*

While I may have not felt amazing, as a human being I am amazing and was perfectly entitled to use this reply, while carefully avoiding promoting the idea that I was happy. Rather than go through the motions of *'I'm fine, thanks,'* the irony tickled me and brought a genuine smile to my face.

The shock of the power of the word was a real wake-up call. The power of *'amazing'* was infectious.

People reacted so positively that the results from those encounters were invariably beneficial. This was wonderful because people left thinking *what a lovely positive bloke,* but it didn't leave them with any realization that they were amazing too. I needed the amazement without any *I*.

And so I endeavoured to eliminate the process of acclimatizing to whom I was talking and find the quickest way possible of greeting everyone with '*We exist and isn't it amazing?*'

I started off by greeting people with *'Wahey!'*

It broke the ice but, let's face it, it's a bit silly.

And then one day, my long-standing friend and performance sidekick Johnny Golden, both a dwarf and a giant of a man, greeted me with a mighty, **'Raaargh!!!'** – which, by the way, he spells *RAAHHH.* Johnny got it from Mike and I keep forgetting to ask where he got it from, but no doubt it was passed down a long line of people exploring their inner warrior, right back to our earliest ancestors.

So there it was, immediately recognizable. What sound could be more raw, deliberate and primeval?

I've been asked on a number of occasions whether there is any connection with the Egyptian God Rah. Well, not consciously but what a fantastic sound to express the first great civilization's labelling of the divine. For them it must have sounded as natural as it did to the first *Dad,* who on hearing his baby gurgle, *'Da da,'* exclaimed, *'He must be talking about me!'*

Raaargh!!!

Deliberate, yet uncontrived, the cry of battle delivered with love and the understanding we're all in this together. What a massive and beautiful word.

Raaargh!!!

Unlike *Aaargh!!!,* the *'Rrr'* sound is deliberate, building crescendo as it summons up the power from below the navel and erupting from the mouth with a big bang allowing the manifestation of creation from those infinite opportunities surrounding us at any one time. Once the word trails off, this momentum is already set in motion.

Raaargh!!! is not a reaction. It is the sound of action, even if you have no idea what it is you're about to do, including nothing at all.

Raaargh!!!

Spreading the word

From then, for about a year or so, I replaced all traditional greetings with the word *Raaargh!!!*

It was infectious. My son started using it on online video games, and soon there were thousands of kids using it as a greeting. My handyman started using it and told me about a friend he'd met at a party who wasn't feeling herself; placing her hand beneath her navel she was saying that she felt she had no strength within her. He told her about *Raaargh!!!,* and they *Raaarghed!!!* and *Raaarghed!!!* then spent the night on the dance floor in an intensive drug-free frenzy, laughing and celebrating the power of *Raaargh!!!* One friend took to it so strongly, he would break out into an infectious frenzy, as if he had just scored the winning goal in the World Cup. We laugh and laugh, often expressing tears of joy.

And then the Barefoot Doctor heard it. He took to the word and started writing about it on his website.

'Make fists and, like a large ape, shake them at the world of pressure and roar RAAARGH!!! for all you're worth.

Then as the day progresses and you find yourself confronted by fear or pressure-inducing information, events or situations, Raaargh!!! internally at them and all traces of fearfulness and stress will dissipate instantly.'

THE BAREFOOT DOCTOR

Messages came in from all over the globe to the benefits of this practice and the Doc was considering writing his next book on the subject, though instead encouraged me to write it.

...but that's another story despite the fact you're currently reading it.

The true magic of roaring the most primeval sound possible was that *The Power of Raaargh!!!* meant something entirely different to Barefoot than it did to me. Connecting to your true self brings new understanding, unique to everyone, just as what it brings will be unique to you.

I have tried to quantify the word many times in many different ways.

While at times there's nothing more invigorating than standing alone on top of a windy hillside yelling an almighty **Raaargh!!!** *(and believe me, I have)*, I don't believe I've ever improved on my first attempt at quantifying the sound as an interactive *Aom.*

Many people are familiar with the practice of Om.

A truly balanced Om is Aom.

Aaaaaaaaaaaaaaaa is the sound of self-expression.

Ooooooooooooo is the sound of focusing on others.

Mmmmmmmmm is the vibration of the balance of unity between I and we, which without opposites, one end of the set of scales drops to the floor, manifesting all manner of problems as they do.

Are you having déjà vu?

The chapter on self-love included the very same.

There is absolutely no difference between I and we, other than the fact that we don't think so.

Boundaries are blurred. If you shrank a submarine down to the size of a subatomic particle, as you journeyed you would find no boundaries while travelling through a person, the space in between and the next person along. In the quantum world there are no boundaries.

> '*A human being is part of a whole, called by us the Universe, a part limited in time and space. He experiences himself, his thoughts and feelings, as something separated from the rest a kind of optical delusion of his consciousness. This delusion is a kind of prison for us, restricting us to our personal desires and to affection for a few persons nearest us. Our task must be to free ourselves from this prison by widening our circles of compassion to embrace all living creatures and the whole of nature in its beauty.*'

ALBERT EINSTEIN

So what are the possibilities when we work in unison, as after all, have you seen how long those credits can be at the end of a movie?

The collective

Together we operate as one perfect organism though fail to notice it due to the limitations of individual perspective, which ultimately are the true cause of *Aaaargh!!!* To show the collective mind in action, consider the following story, which is one amongst many similar examples in the wonderful book, *The Wisdom of Crowds* by James Surowiecki, which describes how the collective has shaped our world.

In 1968 the US submarine *Scorpion* sank somewhere in a 200 square mile radius in very deep water. The seemingly impossible task of finding it was given to John Craven, a junior naval officer. He sought the advice of more than 20 experts, all working in different fields.

This could have been a recipe for a lengthy and fruitless debate had his method not been so inspired. Whether specialists in submarine navigation, engine failure, fuel consumptions, currents or the ocean floor, he instructed all of them to tell him where they thought the submarine was by putting an X on the map and WITHOUT ANY DISCUSSION WITH THE OTHER EXPERTS WHATSOEVER. Using Baye's theorem he found an average, made an X, and said they should look there. The submarine was found less than 200 metres away on the first attempt.

To live in this world and see other beings as different aspects of yourself is wonderful... but at times it can be too incredible to take in.

THE OPERATING SYSTEM IS NOT RESPONDING.
PLEASE RESTART THE COMPUTER.

RAAARGH!!!

That's better. OK, so how about jelly beans?

The investigation into the wisdom of crowds began in the Victorian era by scientists intent on proving elitism. Unfortunately for them they discovered the opposite was true. No single being on the planet can reliably beat the law of averages. There are just so many examples to choose from, but I just so happen to like jelly beans.

If you had a very large jar filled with jelly beans and asked people to guess the number of sweets, the larger the number of people you asked, the more accurate the estimate would be, based on an average of their answers. If you asked the entire planet to guess, it is pretty much a forgone conclusion that the average would exactly total the number of jelly beans in the jar.

Feck me.

Perhaps the collective consciousness is responsible for all matter after all.

Well, while this is all very mind-blowing, and before I need another restart, let's shift from the speculation to the source of *The Raaargh!!! of We* and its application.

The path to self-fulfilment

Having grown up in England, I laughed in disbelief when I read that it was a country in which only one in four people can name the first names of all of their grandparents, until I realized I was one of them. Every single being on this entire planet wants happiness, and while some attempt to acquire it more selfishly, others are thwarted by loneliness.

But it is only ignorance that thwarts our happiness, and there is only one piece of understanding that any of us need to find it. Let's all selfishly indulge ourselves with this understanding of the ultimate path to self-fulfilment.

The path is through compassion.

Did you know people living among their extended family have a lower rate of heart disease despite eating more saturated fat than healthy-eating migrants living in the same town? So, if you don't fancy heart disease, go visit your granny and share some bread and dripping, and if you don't have a family, no matter; you can share it with anybody.

A friend of mine told me his parents had the strongest marriage he knew. He asked his dad his secret and he told him that his mother's happiness was more important to him than anything in the world. His reply is reminiscent of the Dalai Lama's definition of love as: *'wishing happiness for others'*. Presumably my friend's mum thinks the same way and they both contribute equally, in their own unique way, toward a mutually beneficial marriage.

When we were born we were totally dependent. As we grew we needed to learn independence and how to help ourselves. This transformation continues as we evolve from independent to contributor and move up the hierarchy. Our compassion needs to evolve likewise.

In the next scene we'll look at performance *(as what other aspect receives more glory at the Oscars?)*, and the importance of not waiting to attain a particular level before jumping onto the stage of your choice. And so it is with compassion.

The 13th Principle of Raaargh!!!
Strive for compassion for everything and everyone at all times.

As the world is a mirror, opening your heart with compassion is the most effective root to loving yourself.

Our aim is to die brimming with compassion, but why wait? Hence, one of our ultimate goals is not at the end, but in the middle of this movie. There is still a lot of work to do, and sure it's going to get tough and we'll probably get our fingers burned, but the sooner you start, the greater your chances of making your movie the greatest love story ever told.

As the *Raaargh!!! of We* is a massive part in both our movies, together let's dedicate this chapter to the women's peace movement in Liberia, as featured in the superb documentary, *Pray the Devil Back to Hell*.

Those women risked their lives during a time of civil war and helped bring about the fall of dictator Charles Taylor and the election of Ellen Johnson Sirleaf, Africa's first female head of state.

In one remarkable scene, the women (Muslims and Christians) barricaded the site of the stalled peace talks in Ghana and announced they would not move until a deal was done. Faced with eviction, they invoked the most powerful weapon in their arsenal: they threatened to remove their clothes. It worked.

Raaargh!!!

AFFIRMATION
I empower my ideal self through my compassion of others.

The Raaargh!!! of Performance & Play

The quality of your movie is dependent on the quality of your performance, which I must confess is a personal favourite of mine.

On any great artistic collaboration, **everybody** needs to push the quality of his or her performance. While a successful life requires collaboration with others, before we set our sights on them, it is the multi-tasking putting on of so many different hats within our being that we need to consider, within each of which we can push the quality of our performance with the power of *Raaargh!!!*

'All the world's a stage.'

WILLIAM SHAKESPEARE

Life is a circus in which you're required to play one role after another while performing your daily rounds, sometimes juggling, sometimes walking a tightrope, sometimes flying with ease as if on a trapeze and sometimes clowning around in order to keep smiling. To play any of these roles authentically you have to be fully present and confident.

Play provides the mechanics of confidence with the ethos: aim astronomically high and be willing to compromise as you go.

'You can learn more about a person in an hour of play than in a year of conversation.'

PLATO

Seeming while being

In performance and play there's an element of pretending, which sometimes gets the negative label of being *phoney.*

The only difference between being *phoney* and *the real deal* is whether or not people believe in you, which is dependent on whether or not you believe in yourself.

So believe!

A comedian is as funny as their skill in telling the gag. The audience's reaction depends on whether the comedian *appears* to be anxious and whether or not they laugh. Of course a comedian cares about the audience's reaction! They've just learned how to *seem,* that's all.

Anyone can learn to put on a show, and providing they're not trying to force something on someone they don't want, anything goes. Our aim is to acquire the balls or ovaries of train robber with the loving desire to be fair.

Which part of you exactly is the real deal? What am I?

For thousands of years, the greatest philosophers and spiritual leaders and thinkers have explored this question, and the only possible conclusion is, as Sri Nisargadatta an Indian philosopher and guru said, *'I am That.'* As for all the other parts, which you can label, the observer creates what they observe.

So if you behave in the appropriate manner and tell people you already are what you want to be, as the self-development guru Dr Wayne Dyer said, *'You're not being a liar; you're being a prophet.'*

If you *seem* a particular way for long enough you will become it. There was a wonderful 1960s film called *The King of Hearts* set in a small French town during World War I. Everyone had left except for the occupants of the lunatic asylum and they took over the town – *taking on the roles* of mayor, fireman, priest and so on. Never had the town thrived with such harmony as everyone lived out their dreams. Once the other inhabitants returned, the *deluded* patients resigned themselves to playing cards in the asylum again.

Let's live however we wish, while embracing obstacles, which serve to improve the quality of our collective achievements.

The challenge starts in the playground when we're told, *'No, I want to be the princess,'* leaving us resigned to the supporting role. I remember a little girl asking my son if she could be the princess, to which he said, *'Sure! But only if you have a gun,'* which was fine with her, so **Raaargh!!!**

Landing a supporting role is all part of the process – and I mean process – because waving a magic wand and *Ding, now I'm a princess!* is strictly for the playground. Don't wait for someone to offer you a dream role because they never will. Have gratitude for whatever obstacle is in your way because that's exactly what you have to master next, so cheers!

No one can perform to their full potential unless they are willing to take centre stage in their own life.

I'm not saying we should attempt to be the centre of anyone else's life.

Save your supporting (and challenging) roles for other people and get on the stage of your choice RIGHT NOW.

My father-in-law was an extraordinary man who sadly died before I had the opportunity of meeting him. So rather than write about him myself, Marcela lovingly wrote the following:

'He would always say, "It's not just about being, it's about seeming. What's the point of being a good girl if you go out and look like you misbehave? Be yourself and show your better self."

This advice has always been very helpful in many aspects of my life. Little did I know was that what my father was teaching me was how to play the game, the beauty of which was that he did it with so much love.

My father never finished school and didn't come from a wealthy background but knew instinctively that looking like a post-Spanish civil war farmer wouldn't take him very far. So as the youngest of 12 children, with his parents and five brothers dead and the rest in Argentina, he needed to seem.

The first thing he did was to go to a shoe shop and try on a pair of shoes, which would take him where he wanted to go. As he had no money, he ran out of the shop and went directly to the church to confess what he'd done, determined he would return to the shop and pay for them with his first salary.

He borrowed a suit from his brother and left for Madrid, where he turned his sadness into singing in the choir. He knew he'd be welcomed anyway, but with his shiny pair of good-looking shoes he felt the part and started networking. The first thing he did was go back and pay for those shoes before buying a ticket to Argentina where my sister and I were born and where, unlike my father, we had the privilege of private schools and orchestras playing at our birthday parties.

My children can at times seem very wild, but when an old lady was struggling with her shopping recently, my eldest helped her and said to me afterwards, "Didn't I make you seem like a good mum?"

Whether I am, or whether I seem, I have no doubt as to what good sons they're both turning out to be, and how proud my father would have been to know them.'

When you know what you need/love to do (and most importantly *why*) the next part is to put on a show.

We know exactly why we're going on a first date or a job interview, which is why we care so much, and it's not being *phoney* to make sure you have clean fingernails or applied lipstick. In the same way, we make sure the house is as presentable as possible before a viewing by a potential buyer.

Personally, I've taken a lot of inspiration from Paul Arden, an Executive Creative Director in advertising, who said,

'When I mention that I am in advertising, people's instinctive reaction is that you are trying to sell people things they don't want ...

... The priest is selling. He is selling what he believes in, God.

The point is we are all selling.

We are all in advertising.

It is part of life.'

The best and most successful type of salesman is the one who sells people what they want. You're happy, they're happy, everything is rosy and remember to be kind to the planet as you go. Before you can sell it, you need to have it, and in order to get it, you need to create the right image.

Even once you've become it, you still need to *seem*, as being and becoming are both part of the never-ending now.

When Mohamed Ali was interviewed, after he had retired from boxing and was turning his might to philanthropy, he said he wasn't remotely bothered about wealth but it gave him the chance to influence people in areas that were important to him. If someone came to his house for a meeting, they would see the massive gates, the landscaped gardens and fountains, and then – *wow!* – a palace of a house! A butler would show them into the drawing room, as Ali would nervously – and I mean nervously – pace around the room, keeping the guest waiting another 15 minutes until they had firmly got it into their mind that *this indeed was a very important man.* The meetings invariably went Ali's way.

*** EXERCISE 6 ***

Get out there in the big *good/bad* world dressed completely differently to the way you usually dress, whether dressing up or dressing down, and marvel at the different way you are treated.

Don't judge people by appeances but be aware other people will always will be judging you, so make this an opportunity to have fun with it.

It's a laugh! And in the memorable words of Marilyn Monroe,

'Give a girl the right shoes, and she can conquer the world.'

Becoming

Of course it's not all about worrying about how other people perceive you, and with the *Raaargh!!!* of play you tap into the most important aspect of seeming: how you seem to yourself. This brings inspiration to you and others by becoming the person you're projecting.

Worrying about how you seem to others can be a huge source of stress. If a tidy house is something you value – which is wise as it will have a knock-on effect on your organization in other areas – don't just tidy the house for visitors, tidy it for yourself, and dress for yourself, too.

Have fun with it and get all the props you need! Buy a Rolex watch if it makes you feel distinguished or, if you can't afford one, get a *fake* and then get onto the centre stage of your dream role.

Eric Sykes, a British comedian, made a wonderful observation about the difference between an actor and a clown. He said that generally actors learn their lines and rehearse a scene over and over again until they know exactly what they're going to do. On the other hand, and again only generally, a clown rehearses the mechanics of a situation, and when showtime comes they throw themselves onto the stage and see what happens.

That's what I used to do anyway.

This scenario makes a performer vulnerable, as you have to come up with the goods in front of an audience, but it also makes the whole act real, as you feel it!

If I had to scale down from the roof of a giant doll's house as a deranged nymphomaniac hunchback, before kidnapping one of the audience – *I made that part up as I can't actually remember what I did next* – I would rehearse the climbing part in costume merely to understand how it restricted my movements. When I climbed down on the night, for all intents and purposes, I was a deranged nymphomaniac hunchback.

Still within the confines of performance, I took this further in Channel 4's *Ibiza Rocks*, in which I featured for the first two seasons. Dominic Anciano, who was originally an actor, brought his favourite aspects into writing and directing the show. He would write the storyboard and only he knew how all his scenes fitted together. He would set the scene up with actors, sound and cameramen at the ready, and none of us had a clue about what we were about to do. Dominic would then explain the essentials of how the scene needed to start, perhaps with a particular line, what needed to happen and how it would conclude. The actors then improvised the scene with the cameras rolling. Sure enough, the whole thing felt extremely real – at least the audience believed so anyway – and left a good chunk of the population at home believing I was an absolute nutcase for the experience.

So while in real life the cameras aren't rolling, in order to progress we have to put ourselves in situations in which we have to be spontaneous and present. A job interview or a first date for a start, not to mention the opportunities we may be offered out of the blue, based on the performances we put in for all those bits in between.

When you go to a job interview, an important meeting or a date, first listen to what the other party wants. Then throw yourself into the part, feeding from the vulnerability that puts you in the here and now, combining what you love with what they want, and providing it.

Perceptions of you. Which *you* is *the real you*? The angry *you,* when your partner locked the keys in the car an hour ago, or the charming *you* at a cocktail party now?

As *I am That*, I can be anything I want to be and so can you. Believe it, feel it and so will everybody else and, most important of all, enjoy it!

Being conscious and present is the point where becoming truly becomes being.

The blurred line between seeming and being is most enjoyable when we play with children.

When my eldest was little and got into *Star Wars*, I bought him a lightsaber. It was a great toy but the the cardboard and plastic packaging took away from its *seeming* to be real. So I took the lighsaber out of the box, wrapped it in a piece of old red velvet and put it at the bottom of an old chest in my wardrobe before calling him in to tell him.

'Son, there is something I haven't told you. Your father is Jedi. You have now come of age and are ready for me to pass down to you my trusted lightsaber.'

There are tears rolling down my cheeks at the memory of his face when he unwrapped that cloth.

'Keep me away from the wisdom, which does not cry, the philosophy, which does not laugh, and the greatness, which does not bow before children.'

KAHLIL GIBRAN

The Raaargh!!! of play

As adults the *Raaargh!!!* of play needn't stop, and wonderful creations can come from it. I once made a recording with Paul McCartney playing a chainsaw that was so so loud, I had to conduct him, and so smokey it set the fire alarm off.

What a laugh!

The Raaargh!!! of play is infectious, and when the fire brigade turned up to put out the fire, I managed to get them to sing on the chorus!

Play is infectious.

Spread the love!

*** EXERCISE 7 ***

Another brilliant exercise is writing a spontaneous flow of consciousness lyrics, so there aren't any instructions for this exercise except to write as fast as you possibly can, as I am now, and see where it goes!

Start off rambling about whatever you fancy and wherever you choose – in the car or bath, away from people, or not – and don't worry if it starts off with random words – dog, apple, hearty, rinkydink! If two poets write a poem about a tree you will learn nothing about the tree and a lot about the poets. Ideas will just stream in as you make links, which are unavoidable if only you allow yourself to. This is lateral thinking. If everything you do is linear, then there's a good chance you'll miss the point. Make a quantum jump sideways and watch what happens. If you're stuck on a project, don't sit there frustrated; go for a walk, stand on your head or look out of the window as the answers lie where you least expect them.

Spontaneous singing, keeping up a momentum with the rhythm is great training, whether you're a scientist or a milkman. One friend of mine recorded an album then overdubbed every single track as one tune in one go with zero preparation. Brilliant! And the results were, too. The guy's name is Dave Spafford, an acclaimed Disney animator ten years my senior and my greatest teacher on the art of spontaneity. Animation is edited in advance. The animator is given the first and last drawing and then fills in the parts in-between. Almost always the animator breaks the movement down starting with the drawing in the middle then the quarters, then the eighths before passing it to an assistant who breaks it down further. The drawings are then handed to an in-betweener who has drawings 25 and 27, and draws drawing 26. Sorry if I'm going too fast but let's see where it goes.

Spontaneity is channelling and quite different from automatic reactions, though speed kills so if you're stressed slow down your average driving speed by 5mph and, as Gandhi said, chew your drink and drink your food. Anyway, as I was saying, Spaff would animate his scenes and, just like life, he had no idea what would happen next, but the results were invariably hysterical.

I asked Spaff to offer me an exercise for this book and he suggested you use the margin at the side of these pages to create a flipbook and start off with a bouncing flea. He recently told me of a letter he'd received from a grateful mother of one of the children he taught to make flipbooks. Her son has become so passionate about it that every day after school he races to his flipbooks and animates. His dad got the bug to, and races home from work to do the same. The mother told Spaff that son and father hadn't been able to relate to each other over anything, and now they couldn't wait to see each other as they knew what they were going to do.

You see? The joy of spontaneous writing! I'm crying again!

Meanwhile...

Raaargh!!! to approval

In order to turn seeming into being we mustn't allow ourselves to be dominated by worrying about what other people think about us. Fear can cause us to drop out before we even get over the first hurdle and robs us of inspired feeling. I'm not talking about a *'sod everyone else'* approach, but do you think Martin Luther King could have made his *'I have a dream'* speech if he was worried about what other people thought of him?

Don't power your seeming with the need to gain public approval because you can't please everyone and the only approval you require is yours.

Regardless of what you do, you will present love in the form of challenge to someone, just as the Beatles and Elvis had their critics, and John Lennon, Gandhi and Martin Luther King all met tragic ends.

I'm working with a brilliant young entrepreneur at the moment who at 19 made a fascinating observation while discussing a possible business partner. He said, *'He's too keen to please. You can't have jam on everything, so you have to choose what you're willing to win or lose and stick to it and, as life's so short, if other people have a problem with it, then that's their problem.'*

Well, technically I'd say *that's their challenge* but what phenomenal words of wisdom. Listen to the young. In so many regards they know not only what's best for them, but for us too, if only we bothered to ask. After all, aren't we trying to regain the Peter Pan in us?

The key to both – not worrying about what others think of you while presenting yourself to the world – is to break down your inhibitions and know you can both *be* and *become* in public through the *Raaargh!!!* of play. All of us have inhibitions in particular scenarios, but when it comes to our dream role we must jump in regardless.

When the time comes, make your move, because you're moving toward your inspired destiny, and in those moments when you are inspired it is impossible to feel any inhibitions for anything.

The 14th Principle of Raaargh!!!
When the time comes, make your move.
///

Overcoming fear

Stage fright is healthy. Fear means you care and it's the reason why Gurdjieff stressed to his students the importance of doing things in public. He would instruct workshops in singing and dancing in public parks to help his students lose their inhibitions.

We need to be able to express ourselves in more ways than on the top deck of a bus on a Friday night after a skinful.

I got the whole bus singing carols once.

Hobbies in general are a great way of gaining confidence as you strive to learn something you are passionate about, often with people you'd rarely naturally be attracted to. And the more diverse your activities, the more likely it is that you will gain insight as lateral thinking makes the connections, rather than seeing the differences between things.

Overcoming obstacles in play and hobbies naturally evolves to applying those scenarios in life, about which we are passionately negative.

Raaargh!!! is about tension and release.

The *Raaargh!!!* of play is about letting go when we feel tense and applying tension when we feel like giving up.

*** EXERCISE 8 ***

You don't have to go public yet.

Stick on the weirdest piece of music you possibly can.

Don't be the listener or even the musician.

Be the music itself.

Start by lying on the floor and stretching every muscle in your body.

There are no rules; just do what feels natural to you – nobody needs to teach a baby or a cat T'ai Chi or yoga, as their bodies intrinsically know what to do.

Be guided by the sensations created within you and don't worry.

No one's looking.

Not yet anyway.

Then choose the piece of music, which has been the most inspirational to you, and, regardless of whether it is a piece of dance music or not, feel the music; the dancer and the dance as one and the same.

Really push it, not with your mind, but with your feelings and sensations, and if you have any doubt as you do, just shout *Raaargh!!!*

If you think this sounds stupid then you definitely need to do it. Next time you hit the dance floor, don't just go through the motions of moving to the music – though perhaps go for something in-between, especially if you're on the pull.

Eye contact. Another way of losing your inhibitions with others is to become comfortable with eye contact.

In the animal kingdom, eye contact is about hierarchy so if you stumble across a silverback gorilla in the jungle, don't look him in the eye.

For human beings eye contact is often associated with wanting sex or violence, so it is essential to be comfortable with eye contact when you're not after anything at all.

Everyone marvels at the Dalai Lama's mastery of projecting compassion when he says, *'Hello.'*

Of course he has a deep genuine compassion as well as being a master of eye contact and the two go hand in hand.

Everyone is shy of comfort zones they haven't stretched and anyone who appears to possess no shyness at all is usually the most vulnerable because they have learned to *seem* all the time, other than a few adventurous masters who have stretched so many.

As so many people haven't mastered the art of eye contact yet, next time you ask the boss for a raise, don't divert your gaze from their eyes until you get an answer.

There's no trick to eye contact and even the shyest people, which you're not, can master it.

*** EXERCISE 9 ***

Get a partner; anyone will do but ideally choose someone with whom you don't want any sex or violence.

Stare into each other's eyes until you both become comfortable.

Don't rush this exercise. Just be and think of nothing until it becomes enjoyable, then gaze more intensely into your partner's eyes until you penetrate the depth of their soul.

The subordination of the downward gaze is egocentric.

You are superior and inferior to no one.

While we're on the subject of performance, we may as well delve into the X-rated aspect of your movie.

*** EXERCISE 10 ***

To increase communication during lovemaking, sit naked and cross-legged opposite each other. Gaze into each other's eyes while your fingers are pointing upwards and your palms are touching as lightly as possible, and keep this up for about 20 minutes.

This is fantastic foreplay.

Once you get down to it, concentrate only on your own sensations and nothing else, which is the main practical aspect of sexual tant*Raaargh!!!*

While I'm on the subject...

Now, this one may not sound like everyone's cup of tea and it requires a degree of coaxing while this book needs to move on. This is your movie, and what a privilege for me to be a supporting character for a brief spell. But if my suggestion strikes a chord with you, having a go at this one just once will bring very powerful benefits of liberation and communication indeed.

Your call, oh and ***Raaargh!!!***

✳✳✳ EXERCISE 11 ✳✳✳

To eradicate inhibitions, you and your partner masturbate yourselves to orgasm while maintaining eye contact.

Mistake? What mistake?

The next biggie, which can hold us back from achieving our dreams is the fear of making mistakes.

The first time I went to a casting the weather was crap and the office was hard to find. I was nervous and made small talk about the difficulties of finding the place. We like to have a good old moan in these situations because then if we do badly, *poor us,* it must have been because the place was hard to find. Of course when you do this you're focusing on the visualization that you're about to underperform, which means you do. I watched all the other actors arrive and do same thing and, *thank you,* I never did it again – at least not at a casting.

But a dog ate my homework.

Never make excuses!

They create labels.

As serendipity goes, I had a great chat about this with a certain lovely little boy only yesterday morning.

While practising a recorder piece, he coughed whenever he made a mistake. So I asked him to play the piece as badly as possible, deliberately making mistakes, and have a right old laugh in the process. He did and without a single cough. We both laughed as he admitted that there was no connection. It's liberating to admit to being shy about making mistakes in front of other people, and he went to school with the elation of embracing the wonderful world of mistakes.

'The most valuable thing you can make is a mistake. You can't learn from being perfect.'

ADAM OSBORNE, AMERICAN AUTHOR AND PUBLISHER

There is no such thing as a mistake. Only by making lots of mistakes can you programme your brain to automatically take the right route.

Mistakes are the only way of learning. In the meantime, don't worry about the reactions of others and don't feel sad or angry when you're criticized, because that's a form of compliment.

I saw a wonderful interview on YouTube the other day of the Dubstep Beatbox artists Reeps One, who put it like this:

'The guys who tell you, "Shut up ... you look like you're crazy in the head..." if you do something and they're impressed then you know you're progressing, so they're the good people to stick around.'

This process never ends, including when you've done everything possible to prepare and you make a mistake on the day. One thing I always stress to performers is the importance of not panicking if they make a mistake. If a dancer trips and looks embarrassed, the audience will become uncomfortable or laugh. Keep on playing and, if possible, make the mistake part of your performance. If the performer pulls it off, her or she can improve the quality of the performance experience as a whole in the process.

For gaining gold at the Olympics this obviously won't do, though there is new understanding to gain from everything. Other than at this level, I generally find that for a polished performance, 95 per cent of the effort achieves 5 per cent of the results, while the restrictions on time and budget can usually be turned around to create an advantage.

When you know you can handle a mistake, they are significantly less likely to happen and when they do, go Raaargh!!! When you're in the moment, moments of improvisation become quite natural.

Great performances occur when the performer thinks on their feet, puts faith in their knowledge and understanding while pushing the boundaries of what can be achieved. The best part of the future is to enjoy it unfolding second by second.

The Power of Raaargh!!!

Mistakes are hugely valuable, providing we incorporate the lessons learned, and unless you're open to making mistakes you're can't learn anything. Being an expert is about knowing lots of simple things. If you are a cameraman, you will only forget *once* to charge your battery the night before a shoot. By the time you become an Oscar award-winning cinematographer, you'll have made every mistake in the book.

And then you still make mistakes, but when you are fearless of mistakes, it becomes impossible to distinguish whether something was a mistake or not.

Louis Armstrong's solo, which I mentioned earlier, has been analyzed by professors of jazz who have no idea if he intended to create new ideas in harmony or whether he had a lucky accident. When you push the boundaries, as I say, they are the same thing.

I know of a certain a Oscar winning cinematographer who, immediately after shooting a hugely expensive battle scene, which had to be captured in one take, suddenly realized he'd overexposed the film.

Oops!

When the rushes were screened the next day in front of all the bigwigs, he was ready and a master at seeming. Immediately after the overexposed scene was screened, he stood up abruptly and shouted, *'Yes! That's exactly what I wanted!'*

Everyone present in the room gave him a standing ovation.

Raaargh!!!

So what mistakes have I made?

> **'If you reveal your secrets to the wind, you should not blame the wind for revealing them to the trees.'**
>
> **KAHLIL GIBRAN**

I'm not telling but I've made plenty, not to mention the Rock 'n' Roll yarns I have to tell! Do you want to hear the one about how I was stranded in the middle of the desert wearing a dress, with no money, and was rescued by Hopi Indians? Or how about telling you which household name and I adventured across the rooftops of Soho, climbing in through any window wherever a party was going on?

But I'll save those stories for whenever we might meet in a quiet pub.

> **'When you are sorrowful look again in your heart, and you shall see that in truth you are weeping for that which has been your delight.'**
>
> **KAHLIL GIBRAN**

And so...

> **'Be regular and ordinary in your life so that you may be violent and original in your work.'**
>
> **GUSTAVE FLAUBERT**

I'm proud to say that I still make mistakes every day, which is evidence that I'm still learning, and those very lessons learned are the ones filling the pages of this book.

As we only learn by making lots of mistakes, everything we pass on to others is learned through those failures. Don't bang on about your regrets, pass on the lessons, and don't worry about your kids making the same mistakes, just instruct as the need arises with gratitude because they'll make plenty of their own.

They say it's better to regret the things you have done than the things you haven't, but with the Power of *Raaargh!!!*

It's better to make mistakes and regret nothing.

As for any possible negative effect we may have on others, remember it's love in the form of challenge for them and, provided you're willing to learn, you needn't feel guilty for anything!

Take guilt-free responsibility for absolutely everything, and never apologize; it's a winning combo.

Disagree by all means, but don't react.

Be superior and inferior to no one

I remember coaching an aerialist for a show who, despite performing a wonderful routine, pulled the facial expressions of someone waiting for a bus. For a different show, I would have perhaps made it a feature and created a humorous juxtaposition between the mundane and spectacular, and the casual with danger. For this particular show, however, it wouldn't have worked.

I asked the gentleman concerned what it was that he wanted to communicate to the audience during his performance. He replied that he was trying to convey that he was better than they were.

NOOOOOOOOOOOOOOOOOOOOOOOOOOOOOOOOO OOOO!!!

The 15th Principle of Raaargh!!!
You are neither inferior nor superior to anybody else.

The answer to losing your inhibitions doesn't lie in deluding yourself you are superior. All strengths are balanced equally by weaknesses in different contexts. You can never be superior to anybody, just better at a handful of things, just as you can never be inferior to anyone else.

Literally being centre stage in a performance is a humbling and shared experience of love. What a privilege to be experiencing a unifying moment of mass focus being channelled through you!

Performance is a form of communication and, as the poet Ivor Cutler said of art in a radio interview, on a subconscious level you didn't necessarily know what was communicated just that you were being communicated with. The only time an audience is united in their reaction to a performance is when it is universally uninspired. A great performance is one that means something different to everyone.

Here, however, the metaphors with art end because the greatest underlying theme you can communicate is that

we're all in this together. The greatest reward, which comes with the inhibition-free inspiration of doing what you love to do, is that it naturally inspires inspiration in others.

Being a prophet with an astronomical vision doesn't conflict in any way with being humble, provided your vision is as much for your benefit as it is for others'. Telling people what you are does not need to involve making public declarations on what you are going to achieve. If you don't deliver, or don't deliver in a time frame or deadline that is perceivable to the third party, you will look and feel like the wrong kind of fool, though all mistakes are wonderful.

> **'Exaggeration is truth that has lost its temper.'**
> **KAHLIL GIBRAN**

Taking centre stage

Whether to keep it fresh or get ahead, both require putting yourself into situations that you wouldn't usually find comfortable. You remember *The Dice Man*? Don't rely on chance and make yourself the centre of any old stage, choose your dream role and jump on that one.

Get on the stage! If you know which stage then get on it as quickly as possible. Don't put it off and NEVER wait until you reach a particular standard because it is only the experience you acquire once you're on it that counts. And the more mistakes you make, the better, because you'll learn more than ever. Keep on learning by any means necessary as you go.

If only I had a penny for every person who has bought a recording studio with the intention of learning how to use it before writing a song, only for it to sit there gathering dust. For those who want to be sound engineers, give it a go by all means, this is fine, but for people who want to record their own music, then write tunes and work out how to use the studio as you record them. Sure the first recording will be slow and frustrating but the second one won't. You don't need all those buttons. Decide what you want to do and use Google to find out which new button to press as you go. OK, I wouldn't want a doctor to use this approach, but the vast majority of ideal roles work in exactly this way.

When you know what stage you'd love to take, you need to prepare for when your heart pumps with fear, which is really excitement, and then jump into the abyss with certainty of all the incremental stages required to get there.

When Marlon Brando famously turned his back to the audience and had a good old scratch of his bum just as his rival leading actress went into her big speech, he knew where the audience would be focusing. A bit cheeky, perhaps, but proof of his mastery of the principles of *Raaargh!!!* and his ability to take centre stage.

Benchmark standards are set by people afraid neither of making mistakes nor of the competition. As we shall see, we actually live in a *dog feed dog world* and keeping the competition on their toes is an act of love. Whatever the competition is doing, rest assured you can do better than that!

Making your move

Preconceptions cause you to look in a particular direction while the opportunity is behind you. Open your eyes and pluck whatever's necessary as the moment arises.

I remember when a promising and relatively inexperienced harmonica player asked me for feedback. He was self-conscious, cupped his hands and played very softly. And he was *not bad.*

While it is important for a musician to learn scales and breathing techniques, it is more important to understand that music is a form of communication. In a similar way, voice training only improves the way you speak without having any effect whatsoever on what you want to say. Practice is practice, performance is performance, and right now this is it. You're only as good as you are now, so you may as well show how good you are now. The surprise comes when you deliver better than you ever imagined possible. Improving your skills is an infinite process and when you perform to your max, it's amazing how quickly you learn sufficient skills to blow away an audience, even on a bad day.

A master performance = skill + vibe.

If I had to be subjected to only one, personally I'd choose vibe every time, though this is not an excuse not to study.

You're only as good as you are now, so be that good.

He got it, and played again, bringing us both close to tears in as perfect a musical moment as I have ever experienced.

Enjoy and embrace it!

What do you want to communicate to other people: a shared joy or a shared self-doubt?

Don't worry about getting it right, as it is your inhibitions which are causing the block. When you play a *wrong* note or communicate the wrong message, enjoy those moments most of all because it means you must be in the here and now. Then try it again and *WOW* your audience. If they aren't, keep going until they are, because they will be.

Forget about motivation. If you don't want to do something, then don't, but how often do reservations prevent you from unleashing your inspiration and doing the thing you'd love to do?

'Fuck it' has two meanings, and the best one is *'Ah fuck it',* you may as well have a go, leaving you with the experience to say *'Fuck it'* to the parts which didn't work out later.

I remember a brilliant young gospel singer whose hero was Stevie Wonder. When Stevie came to his hometown, he wrote a song for him and recorded it without vocals before spending three days attempting to get the opportunity of singing it live for him.

He made it! The two of them travelled 13 floors in an elevator together as his index finger trembled over the play button.

7th

8th

9th

Aaargh!!!

13th. Ding!

And that was that.

Never even managed to say hello.

How gutting!

Do your preparation and remember:

There is no such thing as a bad move.

So fuck it!

Jump!

You can handle it!

I heard a sad story recently of a marvellous teenager who was starting to get into trouble through petty crime. A friend offered him a job as a runner in the movies, which he turned down! *What a missed opportunity*. It turned out that he was embarrassed because he couldn't read and didn't want to be found out – if only the *'why'* had arisen earlier. For now, let's wish him all the very best as the divine order of the Universe does everything in its power to show him *'why not'*.

> ### 'Only those who risk going too far can possibly find out how far one can go.'
> #### T.S. ELIOT

I worked with a well-known singer last year, who told me an astonishing story. At a time when she was beginning to make a name but wasn't major enough to be invited to the Grammys, she decided to gatecrash the event. Her uncle ran a limousine hire company, so she borrowed a fur coat and was driven in style up to the red carpet. She got out of the car with poise and glamour as the photographers' bulbs flashed a frenzy. *What bouncer is going to demand to see an invitation in that scenario?* So there she was, waiting between

Quincy Jones and Aretha Franklin to be seated, only to end up in the front row watching the awards and various performances.

During the proceedings there was a technical hiccup which caused several minutes' break. In this time, she walked on the stage and filled the awkward pause with a virtuoso performance. Not only was she not interrupted and received with great applause, she was also selected and edited into the TV highlights!

Fantastic!

Man, if someone can do that, you can pick up the phone and push for an interview or ask the boss for a raise.

Raaargh!!!

✳✳✳ EXERCISE 12 ✳✳✳

Stand facing a mirror.

Straighten your spine.

Put your hand on your belly just below your navel because that's where your breath is going to come from.

You know what's coming.

It's time to give it the most MASSIVE *Raaargh!!!* possible.

Having doubts?

That's exactly what this exercise is all about.

Shout *RAAARGH!!!* as loudly as you possibly can until every cell in your body resonates with certainty.

Share that certainty with your neighbours and then *Raaargh!!!* even louder.

*** EXERCISE 13 ***

Only you know if you need to do to this exercise again.

Raaargh!!!

AFFIRMATION

I am superior and inferior to no one as I channel my infinite potential.

The Raaargh!!! of Talent, Time, Work & Money

You can make a bad film out of a great script but you can't make a great film out of a bad one. Our goal of course, when it comes to life, is to make a great film out of a great script. No matter how good an idea or goal is, it still needs to be produced, which is where the blood, sweat and tears come in. The same is true of any book, such as this one.

If a goal is achieved effortlessly, then it is a direct result of hard graft on previous projects or the toils of our collaborators and personal education taken for granted from our teachers, parents and ancestors.

Most of us don't have the advantage of the latter, but the moment you realize your achievements are the result of all the most challenging obstacles you've encountered and overcome, the more your heart will open with gratitude, which will remain with you forever.

Positive visualizations are useful in achieving what you want but they can only have any real effect on someone who is already up for a challenge. For those who aren't, the drawback is the immense pressure and feelings of failure when the old negative thinking crops up and *how long can I keep this up? I must keep going...* as the manifestations remain in the world of their dreams.

Once you are inspired, the 99 per cent of perspiration which makes up genius is the best part, because then you are doing what you love as a Human Being and a Human Becoming.

TALENT IS IN THE MIND EXCEPT WHEN IT'S NOT... *AAARGH!!!*

In a mind dominated by fear and pain, you can only do what you **have** to do, which inevitably means that any task is carried out with ever-increasing levels of reluctance and stagnation.

(U)hhh...

Or even with The Disgust of Ugh!

Raaargh!!!

Getting ahead requires a balance of heart and mind, as passion alone leads to infatuation and ultimately resentment. My father-in-law's incentives aren't hard to imagine with his country ripped apart by civil war and loved ones gone. Most of us, however, are living in an era of convenience rather than survival. On the one hand, we are lucky because we have more opportunity to do the things we want, but on the other hand it's harder to pinpoint why we want to do them.

Intentions

Why drives all our actions and, if it is mighty enough, can overpower inhibitions and leap obstacles. If your incentives are strong enough, nothing can stop you – a mother's protective love for her child being an obvious example.

Anyone who didn't fare well at school didn't have a strong enough *'why'*, and you'd be amazed at how many tremendously successful people did badly at school, Albert Einstein and Isaac Newton included.

> ### 'Winston is a constant trouble to everybody and is always in some scrape or other.'
> **FROM WINSTON CHURCHILL'S SCHOOL REPORT**

I guess Winston just didn't have a big enough *why*, not yet anyway.

Teachers are fond of labelling kids as having poor attention, although it never occurs to them that perhaps their approach is no more appealing than a three-day-old Spam sandwich. Many of these same kids, who apparently can't focus, go home and put in eight hours straight without a loo break on the latest *Call of Duty* on the Xbox.

Passing exams proves you can accumulate large amounts of data, but applying it is a different matter.

While good grades are essential for many academic fields, not achieving great academic results is not the slightest problem for creating a dream destiny. In no way am I encouraging anyone to drop out. In fact, if achieving your dream means going back to school, do it now. We all need to focus on whatever interests us. If you are then great, if not let's keep looking and disregard any labels you have accumulated along the way.

I've always labelled myself as having no sense of direction, but when the *why* is big enough I make sure I'm there. For example, when I landed my first job as a film runner in London's Soho straight out of school...

A classic story in itself, but I have to resist the temptation once in a while.

I knew exactly why I wanted to get ahead in film. Being a runner wasn't my dream job but it was a means to get promoted, and getting lost in Soho wouldn't do. So I studied the *A to Z* and within two days I learned the shortest route from anywhere to anywhere. I redirected my priorities when my *why* was strong enough.

The only requirement of genius is doing what you love to do.

How can reluctance ever compete?

Don't judge yourself or anyone else

The problem is that we are so fast to judge people that we never find out their capabilities. And we do the same thing to ourselves, often based on a mishmash of projections made by other people.

OK, saying talent is in the mind is a tad controversial, but it's a good starting point. When I was a kid, I took guitar lessons with another boy, and I found it way easier to pick up than he did.

Raaargh!!!

Oops. That's the wrong kind of Raaargh!!!

He changed schools and our paths crossed 23 years later when I saw him play a gig and, three days after, we ended up playing together for a spell. *Wow, he could play!* What a songwriter, with the voice like an angel, whereas I sing like a dying cat, not that it stops me. I never imagined he could become such an amazing musician.

Even if various activities come easily to people, often they're the ones who take talent for granted and do something else. The tortoise beat the hare and judging talent at first glance is as accurate as assuming someone is stupid from their appearance or the way that they speak. And as children we do the same thing to ourselves, often based on the projections of others. So don't call a child *'pathetic'*. Don't even say, *'You did this and that.'* It's a tough habit to break, but talk to children in terms of behaviour and never label them. Instead say, *'Giving up on the first attempt is not the way for someone to get what they want.'*

So even if there's no such thing as talent, can everybody play for Manchester United and get an Olympic gold?

Of course not!

A physiotherapist once told me I didn't have the ligaments to make it as a competitive gymnast, but it didn't stop me from doing what I love and flying through the air with the greatest of ease. A giant is at a disadvantage when potholing, just as pigs can't fly but, of course, I'm stating the obvious. We're all different but all those differences are physical, which all adds to the uniqueness of our own perfection.

When it comes to the mind, some of us tend to be more methodical and others more inventive. Either way, both have a place regardless of whether it's classed as an art or a science. Art requires perspiration and science requires imagination.

> **'I am enough of an artist to draw freely upon my imagination. Imagination is more important than knowledge. Knowledge is limited. Imagination encircles the world.'**
>
> **ALBERT EINSTEIN**

Having no talent in music is called being tone-deaf. There are people who are tone-deaf, though the condition is extremely rare. If you took George Harrison's guitar part and put it up a semitone to the rest of the band, believe me, you'd notice. The people you've heard described as tone-deaf aren't tone-deaf; they're tone-dumb, and no wonder.

Negative labels, just like positive affirmations, programme your reactions, which create your reality.

I guess because my dad's an accomplished jazz musician and my mum always sang with great passion, it never occurred to me that I couldn't sing in tune. *(If you're convinced you can't, practise singing in a tiled room – OK, the bathroom – and learn to listen to yourself first as to sing in tune is simultaneously active and passive, which does not come automatically with birth.)* I did believe, however, that I couldn't sing harmonies but with practice I found I could. While our potential is infinite, we need to train our talents, too.

Knowledge and understanding

Whatever you want to do, **make sure you train at something**. You will attract a teacher with the same limitations which you believe you possess. Know your potential is without limits and you'll attract a teacher who thinks likewise and, in the meantime, seek out the best. Once I'd exhausted what I could teach my son on the guitar, a teacher sought him out and made contact via Facebook. How amazing! He turned out to be the only music teacher I know who has no holding for the concept of talent.

All great adventure stories, movies and myths involve a mentor – an Obi-Wan Kenobi or Fairy Godmother. Being a Human Being/Becoming is wonderfully complex, and not everything that gets us where we need/want to go can be found from within.

And it's never too late.

One of the most moving documentaries I've ever seen was the story of a choir in a retirement home in the USA. Their director was a wonderful man, who had the phenomenal ability to push them hard (tension) and know when to let go (release). The egoless performances of those wonderful old timers doing some very unusual, even punk covers of music was as inspiring a performance as I've ever seen. Recounting the collective love between everyone in that hall, audience and performer alike, has brought me to tears again.

Schools place a huge emphasis on the accumulation and examination of knowledge as opposed to understanding. Thinking knowledge and understanding are the same is the thing that tricks us into believing we're not all geniuses.

The noted physicist Richard Feynman put it brilliantly in *The Pleasure of Finding Things Out.* He gave a talk to a large group of physics teachers about why so few children become interested in science.

He looked at the first ever lesson in the syllabus and the questions being asked, and found a familiar pattern to all of them. One example was: *why do the soles of your shoes gradually wear down with use?*

'Good question,' Feynman exclaimed before turning to the teachers' answer book to discover that the answer was friction.

'Friction!' Feynman exclaimed, adding that friction was a definition which shed no more light on what was actually happening than before you learned it. The reason we wear down our soles is because any surface we walk on, regardless how smooth, has tiny bumps, which act like little chisels picking away at the soles of our shoes piece by piece as we drag our feet – an action defined by the word friction.

I remember my eldest son learning how to do long division reasonably consistently and realizing he still hadn't any understanding whatsoever of the relationship between the answer and the question.

I'm not blaming schools. We are in an ongoing process of evolution in which the accumulation of knowledge worthy of instruction, is scattered and trapped within the minds of different people.

Human beings made a huge impact, long before the existence of schools. The problem is that we didn't come with a set of instructions. We are like a Ferrari in the hands of a caveman who eventually manages to get to where he's going, but couldn't get it out of reverse and was severely hindered by the fact that no one had invented the road yet and, after an unfortunate incident shortly after the discovery of the power of fermented apples, resorted to travel by foot again.

We'll get there, and we are doing just fine, so don't *com-blame* if you didn't get the education and training you needed to achieve your goals, yet. Search as far and as wide as possible for the information and training you need, and do it now!

Infatuation and certainty

Being an expert, other than physical restrictions, is about knowing lots of easy things. One of the most important things to recognize is that infatuation is a negative emotion, which means it's a lie. The lie is believing that **the person you're infatuated with has something you don't**.

What you recognize in the greats is an aspect which exists as a potential in you. Once your recognize that you possess their exact same qualities, they are yours.

When you buy your copy of *The Breakthrough Experience* by John Demartini, do *The Quantum Collapse Process* not only on the people you resent, but also on all the greats you admire, transforming infatuation into self-empowerment.

Once you've eradicated infatuation in yourself, nothing is difficult, so don't hero-worship anyone. You are superior and inferior to no one. Astonishing feats only ever appeared that way because they are made up of lots of simple things, which need to be learned one at a time. This is only possible once you accept the actuality of *I can*.

Certainty free from the fear of mistakes is your true nature and is the only tool you require and when certainty combines with those moments in which you're not attempting to *attain* a sense of wellbeing, you find you are experiencing a state of wellbeing.

Lots of simple things

Those people we label as great musicians or scientists, or whatever, found what they loved doing and then put in enough practice so that even on a bad day they could perform better than people were expecting, or acquire a sufficient body of work to warrant the label of '*Great*'.

Anything that appears difficult is made up of lots of simple things.

My eldest son became an expert at the video game *Guitar Hero*. He was an expert because he'd put in the hours. One day at a party the other kids were so blown away with his performance that he felt like a *rock star*. He came home and gave all his video games to his younger brother and picked up the *real* guitar, which had been hanging on his wall for five years. He soon became proficient at playing on one string on the first five frets just as if playing the video controller guitar and learned a few simple riffs. He then learned to do the same on all of the strings. He then learned to move across the strings. He got faster at it.

He loved Slash, so I got the TAB music sheet – which works like a music manuscript but shows where to put your fingers on the fretboard – for 'Sweet Child 'o' Mine' by Guns N' Roses. I told him that once you sufficiently break down the elements then everything is easy.

So my son learned the first eight notes of the solo, then the next eight. Soon he could play the whole tune and performed it to a gobsmacked audience within a few months of starting to play.

Next he learned to improvise because learning to cover a song isn't the same thing. Simple thing, followed by simple thing, *obstacle, obstacle, obstacle,* and within two years and, at the tender age of 12, he can work out most tunes by ear and improvise over Frank Zappa.

Goal!

Ah, but he must be talented.

In no way am I detracting from my son's genius.

He is one, and so are you.

Of course he's a genius; he's a human being and talented at everything, just like you. More to the point, he was inspired. Learning lots of easy things is about putting in the time and, when you're inspired, there's nothing else you'd rather be doing.

Again, if there's something you don't want to be doing, then don't. For me, DIY stands for *Don't Involve Yourself,* but there's plenty of other stuff I do genuinely love doing, while there's plenty of people who love making and repairing things. The point is, when I put my mind to it, I can fix a window just as they could write music or put on a show.

In the same way small children are amazed their parents can drive a car, it just doesn't look like it's made of lots of easy parts to someone seeing the polished presentation.

If you believe something is difficult, you won't be able to do it, so break it into parts you find sufficiently easy to know that you can master them and move on like the tortoise who beat the hare.

The reason children are streamed has nothing to do with intelligence but rather an ability to concentrate. Spend a couple of lessons in a class, among many, chatting or daydreaming and suddenly the next class doesn't make sense (these are often the children that would learn better through seeing or doing). Aside from the assumption of *this is difficult* and therefore *I can't,* beware of labelling anything you find difficult as boring. Everything is interesting provided you are interested, and *oh yes you can!*

Without exception, all skills and knowledge in all fields are simply a case of knowing lots of simple things, which when broken down sufficiently can be mastered provided you're inspired enough to put in the time. If other people seem to pick something up faster, don't even think *lucky them* because it is guaranteed there are other areas of equal significance which you will pick up way faster than them. Isaac Newton lacked social skills, not that he couldn't have empowered them if he had had a big enough *why.*

Raaargh!!!

Once you know what your goal is, make a game of breaking down any areas you think are *difficult* into achievable exercises, and most importantly, incorporate them immediately.

Although it's worth remembering that if you want to achieve grade eight in six months, you can, but the danger is that learning faster than you can incorporate the lessons learned can take away the fun and hinder you achieving your long-term goal. So, often we give up because our goals aren't big enough, and a mid-term goal may not be the path to achieving it. Have a massive goal, a to-do list and be flexible for the parts in-between by always applying the ethos of tension and release.

If you want to get through medical school or be a lawyer, then you won't have the luxury of taking your time, so focus on your true goal, but you may be wise to train your speed-reading and memory skills before you start.

Having tight and loose time pressures has an equal number of advantages and disadvantages. As a musician without any pressure to learn, coming up with labels along the lines of *'Oh I don't want to learn how to play chords as I want to be a lead player'* will unquestionably hold you back considerably, though nevertheless that is what people tend to do.

I know brilliant musicians who take pride in the fact they don't even know the name of the notes on a keyboard and yet never figure out that their main frustration is having to depend on the other musicians around them. This is only caused by the insecurity of *I can't*, whereas without exception, *you can*. And all that stuff about losing the vibe if you study is rubbish unless you confuse performance and practice as the same thing.

I've never found a skill I couldn't pick up provided I had a big enough *why* and I am inspired by the achievements of all the people who didn't appear to tick all the relevant boxes, yet applied themselves with dedication to great effect. This goes for absolutely everybody in absolutely everything.

With one caveat.

Some years ago a friend told me that his dad always used to say, '*You may as well have a go, and only call someone in when you get stuck.*' Armed with these inspiring words, I attempted to veneer the dashboard of my beautiful pink London cab to go with the white walled tyres, crushed velvet interior, massive sound system and blue light, which said RELAX. I ended up shorting out the electrics and having to call someone to rewire them, costing me a small fortune. But so it goes; there are no overnight solutions and that's what keeps it fun.

This book is not about what you're going to do next week. This book is about embracing the inspiration of a life's work in the now and to keep on keeping on. Have a go at whatever you fancy, then you'll be able to refine your choices as you do.

Raaargh!!!

Inspiration is the best motivation

We all have a unique list of priorities of what we value most and least. This means there's somebody out there who loves doing everything that must be done. The things we value change throughout our life, just as sex shoots way up the list at puberty and down when we're having to do the 3 a.m. feed. But many of our values are there at a very young age, some possibly at birth.

Living our dream role is completely dependent on what we truly value.

Often our dream roles are projected roles. Perhaps your parents wanted you to be a doctor or you noticed how being good at team sports made you popular, or you saw the fame and fortune of rock stars having a good time all the time – or so it *seems*.

Respect, popularity, fame and fortune are all by-products of the thing you do and, if your heart's not in it then you're just not going to do as well as you could. If you think you know your dream role, to the point you're constantly banging on about it but never do anything about it, then it's probably one of those which has no leading role whatsoever.

The key to success is through inspiration and the key to inspiration is recognizing your values. There's simply no way everything can be of first equal value to everybody. Our main obstacle is thinking that some things have a higher value than they actually do to us. If your priority is being famous and scoring chicks, then learning to play the guitar to become a rock star isn't likely to inspire your music. You not only need the *why*, you need the *what*. When you know the *what*, it's much easier to achieve your dreams and score whatever you want.

The most important aspect to understand in regards to talent is that it involves something you value sufficiently highly to warrant spending the time thinking about it. If all you think about is food, even if it's by punishing yourself, then you're going to make a better chef or dietician than a lawyer.

If you have no idea of what your dream role is, then the answer lies in it being the antidote for whatever obsesses you the most and causes negative emotions, because it clearly involves something you hold in high value. Suffering is the tool of a loving Universe attempting to drive you to turn it around.

The Power of Raaargh!!!

Once you know what you value – and add to that 1 per cent of inspiration a further 99 per cent of perspiration – then you too can be labelled a genius by others. Nobody's going to pay you to train, so only the people who love what they're doing will be the ones willing to put in the time.

Time

I go off on one on that word, though I'll save it for next time.

For now I'll stick to the point and look at time in terms of putting in the hours.

In Malcolm Gladwell's book *Outliers,* he talks about the 10,000-hour rule. This is the amount of time it takes to become proficient at anything and there are no short cuts. There is also no substitute for keeping going despite all the setbacks.

So at what point does all this passionate sweat and toil pay off by landing that dream role? The pay-off is that you're doing it now, whatever you're doing.

'Here it is right now, start thinking about it and you miss it.'
HUANG PO, NINTH-CENTURY CHINESE ZEN MASTER

On those occasions when miracles do appear with the speed of a magic wand, you simply meet a proportional number of challenges now you have that role, than it would have taken to earn it the long way round.

I've lived a variety of dream roles, which changed hugely when I landed my dream role of being a father.

At this time, I was working as manager of East London's centre for art, education and cultural development, while also touring as a trapeze artist and circus clown. It all got a bit too much, and regardless of how hard I tried, wherever I was, I was always letting someone down. So I obtained a new goal of spending more time with my family while combining art and management by producing large stage shows.

While London was a great place for my work, I went with my gut reaction that moving to Ibiza was a more conducive location for family life, the certainty of which overrode any fears of having absolutely no idea what I was going to do there because my contacts were in London.

The first people I met in Ibiza were a couple who walked into our garden asking if we'd seen their lost dogs. *'No, but would you like a cup of tea?'* It turned out they were Mike and Claire, creators of Manumission, the largest weekly party in the world.

Once I realized who they were, I asked if they needed a flying trapeze act to which Mike said, *'I'm trying to book one at the moment!'*

We had a meeting at the end of which they decided they didn't need a trapeze act and instead employed me as Creative Producer for massive stage shows with up to 50 dancers and 20 circus artists.

How classic that by putting my family first my dream role came out of nowhere!

We'll come back to this but for now I'll say that it never ceases to amaze me the number of times the manifestation itself is provided on a plate *seemingly* out of the blue.

For some reason, however, I've never witnessed it happening to anyone who wasn't in the process of actively doing something about it.

Both lateral epiphanies and manifestations from nowhere require some form of linear process to get the alchemy cranking, which in this instance came in the form of my CV.

Anyway, in terms of landing the career I was after at the time, it's a great story on paper, but life is not about achieving some massive goal in an allotted time and my challenges were by no means over once I'd landed it.

Your true goal is to have one in order to enjoy the process of working toward it as a permanent work in progress. I've been in bands where the only goal was to make it big – making it far less enjoyable and therefore less likely to happen – whereas doing what you love makes any possible pay-offs a mere bonus.

The certainty of your goal is to live happily ever now and to be certain you can conquer all challenges even at the times when it really doesn't appear that way.

This process is timeless.

Abundance

One of our greatest challenges is combining doing what we love while making enough money. The law of abundance states that there is enough to go round and this is achievable because we all want different things. Mind you, it sometimes doesn't appear to be the case when you look at the current strain on the planet and the number of grey-haired actors waiting tables on

Broadway, as well as the massive plethora of bands spending all day promoting their music on Myspace.

This is a very difficult subject indeed.

So I guess I need to break it down.

Appreciate what you're worth. Regardless of whether you are working at doing what you have to do, or doing what you love to do, understand that:

> **'Work is love made visible. And if you cannot work with love but only with distaste, it is better that you should leave your work and sit at the gate of the temple and take alms of those who work with joy.'**
>
> **KAHLIL GIBRAN**

This doesn't mean you should give up the day job. Appreciate what you have and what you have will appreciate all the easier, if your bank balance is at least in black.

Money, like everything, is energy and is the most efficient form of exchange between people. If you have a product or service and need something which someone else has, but they don't want what you have, you're stuffed. And if your need is food or medicine, you're really stuffed.

The negative aspects of money are the greed for power without responsibility and obsession for material possessions that aren't appreciated. Only then is true that, as Kahlil Gibran said, *'The most pitiful among men is he who turns his dreams into silver and gold.'*

Power with responsibility and possessions which are appreciated are worthy pursuits, and for the latter, ask yourself if you really need it, regardless of how rich you may be. If a possession is deeply appreciated – whether sentimentally, practically or financially – then great but if not then sell it, or even better, give it away. If no one else wants it, then bin it and, if you didn't get your money's worth, think more carefully next time.

The only way your wealth appreciates is if you appreciate what you have, so start by knowing exactly what you're worth. This is how the rich make their money work for them while the masses work for their money. Why work like a donkey for the rewards of a handful of grass when fields of the stuff surround you?

On the other hand, making money your only goal, as did the guys at Enron, leads to what many describe as *'evil'*, which is really only ignorance caused by the automatic thought pattern called externalization. In other words, not taking responsibility for the effects our actions are having on third parties. Spiritual poverty without the richness of compassion is the most wretched poverty of them all.

The key to getting it right is fair exchange. The greater the benefits to the greater number of people you can provide, the more money you are entitled to earn, for the simple reason that you are taking on a greater level of responsibility. This comes through valuing yourself, your product or service, your customers, the environment and money itself. Nobody who valued money as a form of energy of fair exchange would consider stealing or attempt to get something for nothing, just as somebody who values their talents would never consider doing something for nothing.

If you value money, you will make it regardless of whether it is through your dream role or not and the best book on money that I've come across is *How to Make One Hell of a Profit and Still Get to Heaven*, also by John Demartini, and also published Hay House, so more fair exchange.

Raaargh!!!

Plot Point 2

Plot Point 2 is the event which turns the situation around for our heroine or hero (you) and reveals a light at the end of the tunnel (a cliché, perhaps, but the process is by no menas over). From now on, it's all about car chases and going firmly in the right direction.

Raaargh!!!

Are you ready for it?

Aaargh!!! but before we can, we come to **the black moment**.

Our hero or heroine was called to adventure (creating gratitude for challenge), which was greeted with fear or reluctance.

They are then encouraged by a mentor (*your Obi-Wan Kenobi or a Fairy Godmother, of which we have many and right now it's me*) but it is not until Plot Point 1 kicks in (Luke Skywalker's discovery that his family has been killed – which for you is *The Script*, and if it lacks the same degree of intensity, don't worry, we still have to look at *the why*) that they are resolved to cross over the threshold and follow the yellow brick road.

Along the way they meet allies and enemies, and Act II, known as conflict, which affects the **choices** they make along the way.

What links all myths, legends and movies is this process including **the black moment**, when it all becomes too much and all is lost as the dream is crushed.

Ever had one of those?

In my ridiculous movie creation with the aliens, the goal of our hero was to get Tammy and his family back. **The black moment** is when he realizes he's been betrayed by Lassie, who is actually an alien scout in disguise intent on taking over the Earth and who has plotted the whole thing, imprisoning our hero in the old tin mine.

This is where The Power of *Aaargh!!!* is at its most powerful, and whether daft crap or a masterpiece, all stories follow this theme.

I wonder why?

But from this deep despair comes Plot Point 2 as something happens that turns the situation around, and our hero's goal becomes reachable. The betrayal of Lassie is the very thing which reveals his family are still alive and imprisoned in the old tin mine, though the challenge is by no means over yet.

Meanwhile, back in your movie...

The heavens are never plotting against you, and **the black moment** is the lynchpin for your success or failure in your **psychological process**. Will you give up or will you be reborn from this ordeal to find the Holy Grail – **an analogy for new insight and understanding** – which needs to be taken with you on the long journey home in Act III – an analogy for **incorporating this new understanding into your life**?

Never overlook the power of understanding, whose gems are actually greater than the physical manifestations on which you're setting your sights and were gained along the way as a direct result of setbacks that wouldn't be possible without a quest. Wanting to think positive 24 hours a day is ill-fated, but understanding this process is unquestionably *win-win* all the way, as you will always either get what you want, or get what you truly need.

Earlier on we looked out how our Universal Plot Point 1 was gratitude for challenge.

So what is the universal Plot Point 2 which shows that light at the end of the tunnel in your movie?

What is the ultimate mantra for scoring manifestations and make your dreams come true, both to be and to become?

Are you ready to get in that car and speed off in the right direction?

Do you believe?

As our lives are a series of beginnings, conflicts and resolutions, we need a Plot Point 2 to call upon whenever it's needed.

'This better be good.'

Are you ready?

'WOULD YOU JUST TELL ME PLEASE?'

Plot Point 2 to bring about all resolutions is: **understand and do.**

'Is that it?'

Yep.

Have a goal, have a go, understand and do, and if you don't know what to do, make a start with something you do know, as that's the only way that new understanding and opportunities can literally jump laterally, seemingly out of nowhere.

Frustrated people experienced in taking action need dreams and frustrated dreamers need to take action.

The more of a revelation, the less effective Plot Point 2 would be, because if it worked *that* well, you'd have heard of it, which you have. There's no secret to getting what we want in life; you get out there and just do it.

Of course when you're working toward something you love, loathing doesn't come into it, though I guess I've mentioned that one. Focus on the most massive dream of dreams and what you can, and ultimately are **doing** right now, and embrace the mystery of what's in-between.

Start by writing a to do list, cross off the ones you've done and carry the ones you haven't done over unless they become obsolete.

Everything in this book is about increasing your understanding of your ability to do. Regardless of whether you focus on the goal, the team, the opponents, the crowd or the after-match drink, none of it makes much sense unless you are at least up for running about and kicking the ball.

The 16th Principle of Raaargh!!!
Understand and do.
////////////////////////////////

As we approach Act III together, prepare to jump in your Mustang for that final car chase. Now you are going firmly in the right direction but ease off on the gas, take in the scenery and flick on the radio as it plays the current overture of the symphony of the orchestra of the Universe.

You've got all the time you'll ever need.

Love is timeless.

If Plot Point 2 lacked a little in sensational spark, remember those lateral jumps of epiphany and manifestations which are born from a linear process of understanding and doing.

The best is still yet to come, which of course is the realization you already have it.

The following affirmation is my personal favourite and was passed to me by Demartini who learned it from Dr Paul Bragg, an author and pioneer of wellness in America. It is the greatest gift you could pass on to anybody, too.

AFFIRMATION
*I'm a GENIUS and I **APPLY** my wisdom.*

ACT III

'There's no place like home.'
L. FRANK BAUM, *THE WIZARD OF OZ*

The Raaargh!!! of Living Happily Ever Now!

Act III is known as Resolution.

In Act I we got a taste of the part of life you want to leave behind and Plot Point 1, the goal you'd love to score and the Universal Plot Point 1 of gratitude for challenge.

Act II was the struggle to overcome all the obstacles and ended with Plot Point 2, which revealed a clear shot at the goal.

So Act III comes after that black moment of doubt and you're now racing in that car in the right direction to bring about the resolution. The destination will become the beginning of the next phase in your life.

When new movies are screened to a test audience, the part most likely to get a re-edit is the ending and sometimes they even reshoot it.

The Power of Raaargh!!!

Got to get that right.

And they all lived happily ever after...

We love happy endings because in the *real* world, one situation always rolls into the next. We are caught in an unending journey toward living happily ever after.

What are you waiting for?

THE END?

There are no happy endings, just happy nows

Living in hope of a happy ending reaffirms that things are not OK now.

Instead, we think that everything will be OK when *[insert your own happy ending here]*.

If and when **WHEN** ever comes, you'll discover that you're still in the middle, and everything will only be OK when... and the cycle of waiting for resolution begins again.

Imagine suddenly waking up to find yourself somewhere over the rainbow, in a life in which all your dreams have come true.

Would you feel self-fulfilled?

No you wouldn't.

We love the idea of pushing a magic button that would make all our dreams come true.

Does the person who climbs Mount Everest see the same view as the person dropped at the summit by helicopter, or better still the same one you can see on TV from the comfort of your sofa?

And how about that bloody National Lottery?

Oops. Not voicing negative reactions is a work in progress for me, too.

Lottery winners get used to their new lifestyle like the Arctic polar bear, relocated to a zoo in Australia. Once he acclimatized to his new lifestyle, he refused to get in the pool unless it was heated to a minimum of 15 degrees. Without any goals, I think the polar bear was trying to tell the crowds, *'Err, I can't be bothered.'*

I'm not saying money is a bad thing. It's the most efficient energy of exchange between people, but where's the exchange in winning the lottery?

Greed doesn't prevent successful businessmen from retiring. They are successful and don't retire because they are doing what they love and thrive on challenge.

Imagine wanting to have a son who was a doctor...

CUE – Puff of smoke.

There he is!

You didn't have to go through any of the nappy changing, teething, crying, colic or cuts and grazes. Instead you could have gone where you pleased, when you pleased, no arguments, sleepless nights of worry, teenage rebellion or broken hearts and, *wow,* look at all that money you saved!

And yet here he is.

My one's called Dr Holden.

Hello, Doctor Holden. Allow me to introduce myself. I'm your dad.

Ah, but of course... It appears we don't know each other.

Our satisfaction from the manifestations we create is drawn from **ALL** the experiences of how we made them. These are your current struggles and, as such, this is how it is possible to be grateful for them.

Just because it doesn't seem that way when little Johnny is screaming at the top of his lungs at 4 a.m. in the morning, doesn't mean we won't look back from a cosy fireside with gratitude later. We need gratitude for our struggles NOW in the shape of *gratitude for challenge,* which becomes so much easier once we realize obstacles and opportunities are one and the same.

Once you achieve some degree of happiness, you encounter new obstacles. If your only goal is for the obstacles to go away, then you're in deep poop, because they won't.

If you continue to have goals, obstacles will always be here to serve you.

Do you still really think that once you've achieved your dreams everything will be OK? If you could create the perfect life without challenge it would be so boring you'd have no other option other than to invent some.

When children play, nearly all of their games are about achieving tasks and inventing obstacles to overcome. Kids know what it's all about, and Darth Vader action figures outsell Luke Skywalker by the boxload. This is not because we're drawn to the dark side. It is because we're drawn to obstacles as springboards to jump into the light.

Creativity needs something to rebel against.

After throwing TVs out of hotel windows had become more than a little jaded, The Gaye Bykers On Acid took cleaning products and a vacuum cleaner on tour with them and left dressing rooms way more immaculate than when they arrived.

Rock 'n' Roll!

Keep it fresh, keep it new and keep on playing. Welcome your obstacles and be grateful. It is the keeping going, not the achieving of our goals, that makes life worth living. Goals are designed to keep us in the here and now, and to stop us from projecting wildly into the future.

Planning too many moves ahead in chess is a great way of losing because you will waste time focusing on moves your opponent is almost certainly not going to make. Keep your defensive and offensive positions strong and enjoy the surprise of how the game unfolds. This is playing to win and being *happily ever now.*

A sense of direction

Goals exist in order to create a direction in which to gather momentum. Once you're moving in the right direction, achieving your goal is merely a bonus as we traverse joy and sorrow and runs of *bad luck* and periods of thirst for self-perfection.

When we live like this, we stumble across realizations that some of our goals are illusions – a resolution in itself. We re-evaluate, set new goals and set off that way.

It's a blast.

The amazing part of living this way is the amount of times you score without having to try, like a goalkeeper scoring a goal when he was simply aiming to wallop the ball up the other end.

Last year I was asked to work with a well-known music act that was about to start their third comeback in over 20 years with a re-release of their only hit. Clearly they needed to write some new material. Instead they asked me to organize a huge spectacular show based on the solitary famous tune.

Well, OK then.

I organized a world tour, sourced dancers, a choreographer, acrobats, lighting, projections, props and costumes and, most importantly, venues. No idea was too ridiculous or extravagant and was abandoned only when we couldn't get it to work. We laughed and laughed, and then laughed some more.

My client became excited by the show and, free from pressure, began writing bits of incidental music. I suggested turning one of them into a single and we found the perfect singer for the job.

The show proved too expensive and was shelved, but the act didn't need any frills to sell out big venues any more because their new song became one of the biggest hits of 2009.

When you're in harmony with what's going on around you, treasure pops up in the most unexpected of forms.

Appreciate what you have NOW

The law of attraction states that real and positive affirmations work, but only if you understand them. Sitting on your behind visualizing cheques coming through the letterbox is most likely to attract a life of sitting on your behind and a steady stream of bills. This is because it involves living in hope of a happy ending, which means you don't appreciate what you have **now**.

If you appreciate nothing, you'll receive nothing, unless of course you do, in which case you won't appreciate it; it's proportional.

Imagine two young people working in McDonalds. One is grateful for the opportunity of earning some extra money while pursuing their dream at the Royal College of Music, while the other can't wait to clock off and get on the Xbox, drink a beer and put on weight while fantasizing about becoming a professional footballer. Then there's the guy who doesn't work anywhere and talks about going to the Royal College of Music if only he could raise the money.

Which one do you think will manifest their dreams?

If you want your dreams to come true, wake up!

Wanting a happy ending is searching for happiness, which as the good old Buddha said, was the root of all misery.

The 17th Principle of Raaargh!!!
Live happily ever NOW!
///

Don't yearn for a happy ending.

Look for a happy **now**, and if what's happening now is a bit rough, then clearly you're still alive.

True and wonderful!

If you're very, very pissed off, then do Exercise 2 or take a peep in your gratitude book and start a new beginning. Your future will be the outcome of the accumulation of how present you are **now**.

There are no endings like the ones that happen in movies. Everything is overlapping, and we are permanently in ACT I, II and III simultaneously.

Life is a series of goals, which makes it a series of obstacles, every one of which is unique.

Everything is a series of new beginnings

We can only return to the same place if we have learned nothing from the experience and it is only our mechanical thought patterns that lack creativity.

In Gary Zukav's excellent book, *The Dancing Wu Li Masters,* he demonstrated this idea by naming every chapter, *Chapter 1*. Written in the late 1970s, Zukav compared the twentieth-century's understanding of quantum physics with ancient Taoist teachings.

Both schools agreed that the Universe was in a constant state of change: an endless stream of beginnings in which experience is often applied out of context and you'd be better off in many cases knowing nothing at all.

I don't know.

Experience, by its very nature, can't produce anything original; only new experience can do that.

Yeah, great, but my life is so boring, mundane and repetitious. I never have new experiences.

Is that you?

We don't need motivation to do what we love, and the only time your life is repetitious is when your thinking is repetitious.

In my younger days, when I first became interested in meditation, yoga and diet, I shared a house with five people. My goal of eating healthily was thwarted daily by my aversion to washing up and every plate, pan and utensil was permanently dirty. It was grim.

The mere sight of piles of washing up filled us all with *The Power of Aaargh!!!* and we lived off takeaways. If only there was a button I could press that did the washing up *(now I've got one)* so that I, at least, could live happily ever after.

But boy did I lack motivation.

Start

I checked my posture and made sure bending forward over the sink was done in a way that was beneficial to my spine.

I made it, but still not enough of an incentive; surely there's something more for tomorrow?

Restart

I drew inspiration from the movie *Cool Hand Luke* in the scene where the prisoners worked as fast as possible laying tarmac on the road, giving them the rest of the day off.

Still not enough of an incentive. Next.

Restart

I washed up like an extreme skier: no two wipes were the same. There is no repetition of movement, merely our own repetition of negative reactions.

Sorry, still not enough.

Restart

It made me laugh to wash up with gratitude to the bowls and spoons, as eating soup without some kind of container sucks. After all, all matter is also manifested from the spiritual domain, just like us. I genuinely began to develop an appreciation for those cheeky plates.

Good one, but still not enough. How long can I keep this up for?

Restart

Then it dawned on me that my previous irritation toward my housemates was unjustified as they did 100 per cent of their own dishes, as they had no other choice with everything constantly dirty. It occurred to me that since birth I'd probably done the dishes for only about 5 per cent of the meals I'd eaten.

I began to do the dishes every morning out of gratitude to my mother.

Sorry, Mum – it still wasn't enough of an incentive; surely there's something else?

Living in a tidy house wasn't high on my list of priorities at the time. I just didn't notice the mess, and finding the motivation to do something I didn't care about just wasn't going to come.

Fuck it (release).

Restart (tension).

So what was my motivation in the first place?

The answer was obvious and I went back to the start.

I was inspired by my new experiences of diet, yoga and meditation and knew that when I focused on them, without any conscious analyzing, everything else fell into place. This prospect excited me and when something excites you, you don't need any motivation at all to muck in with the stuff like the shopping and cooking of good food.

There was only one obstacle standing in my way. Having a tidy kitchen was the only hurdle I needed to leap in order to score. The washing up was an easily achievable opportunity to have what I wanted.

I focused on the *why.*

Without saying anything to anybody, I just got on with it.

Nobody appeared to notice.

Nobody said anything and nobody thanked me, though I had the last laugh as I put it in this book.

Within a month everybody was shopping, cooking and washing up afterwards, bringing new meaning to *you need do nothing* once living in an environment in which there was nothing quite so glaring to do.

My objective was to have a kitchen that would inspire the creation of nutritious meals. Everything else was secondary and achieving it involved steaming into mundane tasks. Looking for motivation sucks because it means focusing on something you basically don't like doing.

When you focus on what you love doing, it never occurs to you that all the jobs you have to do to make it possible are a drag. This is what gives us momentum to keep going, creating more gratitude for challenge in the process.

All you need

So how about your timeless movie?

Have you ever noticed what *The Wizard of Oz* is about and why it has stood the test of time, echoing a theme which has been rife in all cultures for thousands of years?

Dorothy's Plot Point 1 was to find her way home, just as the Tin Man, the Lion and the Scarecrow were all seeking qualities they already possessed, though without understanding and doing, had never previously realized.

There's no place like home.

Dorothy awoke to the realization that everything she experienced on the other side of the rainbow was everything amongst which she was living on this side.

For the rich and poor, the famous and the unknown, the resolution all of us are seeking is for our hearts to open in a state of gratitude for what we have right now.

We love to see it in the movies as we yearn for it at all times. All of us experience moments of gratitude but, confusing our finger with the moon, we don't notice the true prize is the state of gratitude rather than whatever triggered the experience. Don't be greedy for all that stuff; be greedy for gratitude itself.

All we need to do is to count our blessings, embrace challenge as a state of presence, have a goal, and understand and do – while seeing all the bad days as opportunities as part of the process to enable us to minimize those gaps of ingratitude within a Universe in a constant state of transformation.

Gratitude and *a state of presence* for challenge is all you need.

Gratitude is what keeps us present as a *Human Being*, while fulfilling our role of *Human Becoming* as we evolve from dependant to contributor and beyond.

And here we come to the main theme in this book, and the most important *Principle of Raaargh!!!*

The 18th Principle of Raaargh!!!
You are, and always will be, a work in progress.

So forget the happy ending!

Forget even being happy now because as soon as you start thinking about it, you are missing the fact that *it* is **happening right now**.

Just zone into those sensations in an ever-present wonderblast by keeping on keeping on, working toward and doing the thing you really love to do among the serendipity *doh dah* of it all.

So what are we gonna do about it right now?

Well, for a start, your script will always be a work in progress too, so now's as good a time as any to dig it out for a second draft.

Raaargh!!!

AFFIRMATION

Everything I could ever possibly desire is already fulfilled within me RIGHT NOW!

The Vision of Raaargh!!!

The beginning of the movie was the end of the old, and the end of the movie is the beginning of the new. We love endings most of all, as in life one scenario rolls into the next since the challenges never end.

While your movie is a never-ending story, this book is not, as the thickness of pages to the right of the future is dwarfed by what we have experienced together to the left.

So what's it to be, the aliens thwarted and a reunited family? New love walking hand in hand into the sunset? Or what is it exactly that takes the fancy of yours truly?

> *'To understand the heart and mind of a person, look not at what he has already achieved, but at what he aspires to.'*
> **KAHLIL GIBRAN**

Set your aims high

Both my sons have always had a good head for insight.

The Power of Raaargh!!!

My youngest turned round to me, a few weeks before his second birthday, and said, *'Dad, you're fecking stupid!'*

It's very important for a child to understand boundaries, so I puffed up like a silverback gorilla and said in the firmest way possible, *'Don't you dare speak to me like that!'*

So he smiled from ear to ear, gently punching me on the chin, and exclaimed, *'OK, Dad. You're fecking great!'*

So last week I consulted him as to what I should write about in this book.

He told me that I should tell everyone to aim higher than they want to achieve, as we usually come in slightly lower.

Spot on!

He knows this because his teacher said that if you aim to get 80 per cent in a test, you'll get 60 per cent, so if you want 80 per cent you must aim for 100 per cent. Only by studying beyond the syllabus can you get 100 per cent.

In the same way, when you see someone attempt a back somersault on a trampoline, they're aiming to get round far enough so as not to break their neck, which means that usually they land on their knees. Some people go on to make it because they learn to start the rotation as soon as they take off, although no one can do a double somersault like that. As anything *difficult* is a matter of breaking it into lots of simple things, the first thing to learn is to jump as high as possible and not think about the rotation just yet – you do this by practising back drops with only a quarter rotation.

Aim higher than you ever dared imagine and anything you desire becomes feasible.

The flaw of Aaargh!!!

I remember an interview with Krzysztof Kieślowski, the director of the sensational *Three Colours Trilogy*. He *seemed* to be rather a depressed old man and described his life and work as failures because he hadn't achieved his vision.

On first realizing the perfection of the Universe, I had a similar experience and felt all my work was futile. I spoke about it despairingly to a friend. He asked me to shut my eyes and we went on a long drive, during which I meditated. Once we'd parked, my friend led me inside a cavernous room and asked me where I thought I was. Aware of the perfection of nature and feeling the power of the place, I said, '*We are in a massive underground cave and I'm going to open my eyes to see the breathtaking stalagmites and stalactites; a room filled with the beauty of perfection of nature whatever that may be.*'

I opened my eyes and it was truly breathtaking.

I was in an old abbey of the most perfect architecture and construction, charged with the reverence and power of generations. The abbey had taken 100 or so years to build, which meant the architects worked with dedication and love while aware they would never see their part of a collective vision.

It was a moment of revelation and love, and it gave me the resolve to contribute to this vision – the collective working together to achieve an inspired vision for the future.

I love you, Jamie Kelsey Fry.

Just as the olive farmer plants his trees in the knowledge they will only bear fruit for generations to come, **no endeavours are in vain**.

Similarly, a well-known singer-songwriter told me, in a moment of despair, that his work was like the tiny drips which make up stalagmites over thousands of years, and insignificant as he knew he could never create a stalagmite.

'But don't you see? Your contribution is massive in a unity of infinite perfection.'

Whatever your vision may be, it is part of the collective and the collective is infinite. Not having any vision – no matter how modest it may be – is to feel isolated like a drip in a cave.

Feel love for the collective and obtain joy through mucking in with every drop of strength when it's time for your shift. Relish those moments of doing nothing as you are aware that someone else is doing their bit. Sometimes walls fall down and need to be rebuilt, but take inspiration from the ants that immediately set to work repairing any damage to their shared home.

The greater your vision and the harder you work on your shift, the greater the love, gratitude and joy you will experience from what we are all making together.

This is true inspiration.

Aim astronomically high with your vision, for there is never any compromise in what is achieved, as the ongoing collective is constantly spiralling with an unstoppable infinite momentum.

If in the beginning there was nothing, the creator could only have made us out of Him/Her/Itself and each and every one of us is an aspect of the divine trapped in space and time. And if there was never a beginning, then our existence and ability to create are even more mysterious, though no less miraculous.

We are divine beings.

'Beauty is eternity gazing at itself in a mirror.'
KAHLIL GIBRAN

*** EXERCISE 14 ***

Go and look at the most precious manifestation of the divine in the mirror until you laugh or cry with the love and inspiration that only the divine can create.

Next time you look into the eyes of another person, know that the divine is looking upon different aspects of Him/Her/Itself.

How can this possibly be put into words?

Raaargh!!!

This most basic sound possible is from the source of creation.

Raaargh!!! is like a nano-meditation; use it to connect you to the now and the divine beauty of the collective – ourselves and everything around us.

Understand that the silent **Raaargh!!!** is either to look into the eyes of another person with the knowledge that you are the divine looking upon different aspects of Him/Her/Itself, or the resonance while alone and simply being, while being everything.

So don't aim for 100 per cent.
Aim for infinity as is worthy of your true divine nature.

The only tool for manifestations is to **understand your incentives**. If the *why* is great enough you are unstoppable. Necessity out of a need for survival is a mighty incentive. The ultimate *why* is your desire with absolute certainty to connect with both who you are **now** and all of the infinite possibilities that lie ahead.

The Infinity Principle of Raaargh!!!
The Universe is infinite and universally perfect, which of course includes me.

Competition

Be grateful for challenge and understand that the competition and mistakes you make along the way are the very things that get you there. Aspire to being a work in progress with an astronomical vision, and you're already there.

It beats watching *soaps* anyway.

It's not all about fame and fortune either. We push boundaries with our mind, our bodies, our spirit, our vocation, our finances, our family, our friends, our social standing and contribution to the world as a whole, so wanting to exist in a permanent state of wellbeing is an astronomical vision in itself, which means there is room for everything, including *soaps*.

When you are inspired, you become inspiring, encouraging other people to do the same.

John Lennon hadn't written anything of great merit for a while and one morning heard Paul McCartney's 'Live and Let Die' *(I think)* on the radio.

Wow!

John said in an interview that on hearing it he immediately got out of bed and, shortly afterwards, released 'Imagine'. This is love, and both songs contributed massively to the quality of the collective experience.

You can do better than that!

Are you ready?

Do you believe?

Shout as loudly as possible, 'I believe!'

Hmm, I like that. I'm getting all Gospel on you, baby.

I feel a sermon coming on.

So come on everybody, with flowers in your hair, take the hand of the person sitting next to you as if you were asked at a funeral, and squeeze it real tight. Don't wait for somebody to die before you tell 'em you love them, even if you've never met them before because by the time the future's happened, it's already the past and right now the time is NOW!

So where was I?

*** EXERCISE 15 ***

Get a modest sum of money together and go to the shops, and on the way *don't you worry 'bout nobody*. Nobody's a nobody; nobodies don't exist.

Shout *Raaargh!!!* as loudly as you possibly can and if you feel self-conscious, pretend you're calling out to somebody over there who has the misfortune of being named *Raaargh!!!*

Call them a few times before opening your arms with the certainty that you can aim to infinity. Tilt your head back and open your eyes as wide as possible, shouting the almightiest, infinite *Raaargh!!!* possible directed up toward the heavens and beyond.

Buy a journal you can cherish, a magical book of great importance on which you wouldn't dare put a coffee cup on because it holds a far greater value to you than the table it rests on.

Buy a book that is significantly thick enough to represent the many years you have ahead of you, although, like the practice of some monks who turn their cup upside down so as not to be of inconvenience to others as it gathers dust should they die in the night, allow this book to transform every day into how you would live if it were your last.

Buy a pen to match, fit for writing before the invention of the printing press, and be prepared to write with the same artistry as if you were painting the ceiling of the Sistine Chapel.

In your book, write down everything that you think and feel, and everything that you are and what you will become. It is a book of dreams that will save you years in understanding what you are, taking you further than you ever previously imagined. And if your goal is going to sleep with the lights off, this is achieved through the powers of infinity.

The purpose of this exercise is to explain that thoughts are like steam and easily disperse as one tangent leads to another, while the pieces of the jigsaw puzzle remain scattered. Writing them down transforms your thoughts from steam into a fluid but containable water, on the path to creating a solid reality.

Are you ready?

Do you believe?

*** EXERCISE 16 ***

Shout as loudly as possible, *'I believe!'* RIGHT NOW and get up them shops as fast as you possibly can.

EXERCISE INFINITY

This exercise isn't numbered in the traditional way because it's a permanent work in progress to refine and add to as you cast the old ways away. It is the beginning of a library of books whose first volume is *The Book of Gratitude* that you've already started.

Well, you didn't think I was going to suggest you try to live happily ever after, did you?

#1

Start off by listing everything you can possibly remember that has ever inspired you and all the games you ever loved playing as a child.

Remember those moments which gave you the same feeling as the night before Christmas when you were six, and then move on to anything that invoked the same feeling from any point in your life.

The more detailed it is, the more certain it will become that you will source and then do something that you love to do if you're not already.

It's not a coincidence that I liked dressing up at a time my brother was given chemistry sets. He later became a doctor of physics turned paleoclimatologist using mathematical models of the Earth to unravel the mysteries of the ice ages at a time I was working as a circus clown. This is why the *Raaargh!!!* of play and hobbies is so important both for children and adults, as you can keep doing what you love as you earn money with gratitude. The reaction to this is often that people feel they are far too busy to have a hobby, but the ant never feels busy, which can only be the result of a busy mind easily calmed through gratitude, understanding and doing.

For now, start with your childhood when your responsibilities rarely got on top of you. Perhaps you were inspired to organize a chess tournament or join a drama group? Perhaps you loved bees or dinosaurs?

Whatever it was, write it down!

Read on, by all means. But when you make these lists, take your time. You have all the time in the world.

#2
Now list all the movies, music and art that have ever inspired you and the reasons why.

I'll never stop using metaphors from my passions just as I suggest you never do either. We are attracted to movies in particular for one of two reasons. First, we're attracted to behaviour which we do everything possible to avoid, such as that seen in horror movies. That's fine, provided that you keep on avoiding it! Often the scriptwriter is being very generous as they delve deeply into themselves and the complete picture of the workings of man.

'The wise man learns from others, the fool from his own mistakes. However a wise fool is generous enough to allow others to learn from his failures.'

NASRUDIN

The other type of movies that attract us are

the ones that, while also echoing the words of Nasrudin the greatest of wise fools, also involve triumph in the face of adversity through a level of inspiration and action. The reason we don't mirror this behaviour is because we are distracted by our negative reactions that camouflage *our Why.*

Hmm... perhaps it was a bit of a mouthful, though no harm in that.

As a work in progress, I suggest you list all the movies, music and art that have inspired you and continue to inspire you. It is also wise to always broaden your scope by sourcing gems from the archives, which aren't currently fashionable.

As a kid my three favourite movies were *Harold and Maud, The Graduate* and *Silent Running,* and my favourite song was 'Across the Universe' by the Beatles. All of them meant as much to me as an adult except *Silent Running,* and the key lay there. So why was I so inspired by this one? It was an amazing moment when I realized all three films were about the same thing. They all involved a main character who encounters disapproval from the other characters but meets the approval of the audience. They then have a relationship with someone who's on their wavelength (in *Silent Running* it was three robots) and from then on, nothing was gonna change their world.

My life's work began before I even made the connection that all these moments of inspiration from art – where feeling dominates over thinking – were about not allowing the opinions of others to prevent me from doing what I loved. In my younger days this took on a rebellious, iconoclastic and sometimes destructive path. But, as I evolved from dependant to contributor, has transformed into wanting to encourage others to do same, having chewed the food so you can swallow it more easily, which is exactly what *The Power of Raaargh!!!* is all about.

What connects the things that inspire you?

The key lies there to your *what* and, even if you already know your dream role, to your *why*, right there.

#3

Now list all the greats, and all their feats, in history who have ever inspired you.

The feats of these people are mirroring the qualities you see in yourself.

#4

Now list your perfect lifestyle.

This has nothing to do with your dream role, fame or fortune.

This list might include things like stimulating conversation, enjoying nature's beauty, freedom of movement and creative expression.

A truly fulfilling life is one that is filled with everything you hold of value, whereas success is a term usually applied to how you appear to others. Award winners are rarely the people producing the finest work or the most content. Find a way to be successful at doing what you love and, as you go, recognize you are surrounded by what you most value. You are already truly rich within and this goes for the financially rich and poor alike.

This list creates *the why*, and when you find all the

connections between *the why* and the previous list of *the what*, you will naturally find *the how*.

#5

Now list all the areas in your life where you already have everything in the previous list, in one form or another.

You do.

Only once you appreciate you already have everything you need right NOW can you manifest them into any form you desire. It's the same when looking for the perfect partner. Only once you're grateful that everything you want is spread between the different people currently in your life can you attract those qualities in a single person. Any shortcomings you have experienced in previous relationships are mirroring your own shortcomings, which you need to overcome to create harmonious relationships.

This happens because the parts we don't know or like about ourselves are those we seek in a partner, albeit subconsciously, to fulfil them for us. But they are not your other half; they are another whole with a natural tendency to awaken that dormant quality within you.

If you want your partner to be more devoted to you, ask yourself whether you are being neglectful, too. They say you can't change people, but watch how devoted your partner becomes once you become grateful for them.

'Love one another, but make not a bond of love: let it rather be a moving sea between the shores of your souls.'

KAHLIL GIBRAN

#6

Now list the benefits of your goals; freedom is a great place to start. Don't just think in terms of wealth, which is not necessarily visible or tangible to others, so also include the benefits of the following.

The *Raaargh!!!* of joyously doing what fulfils you.

The *Raaargh!!!* of the joyous connection with your body.

The *Raaargh!!!* of the joyous connection with your mind.

The *Raaargh!!!* of the joyous connection to others.

The *Raaargh!!!* of joyous harmony within your family.

The *Raaargh!!!* of wellbeing and the joyous connection with your spirit.

And of course:

the *Raaargh!!!* of joyous loads of cash.

For this last one, perhaps best not to go off indefinitely on all the wonderful things money can buy. List a dream house, a great education and dream holidays by all means, and the more detail the better, but listing every last thing you want to buy will reinforce the view that money represents things, which it doesn't, making it more likely it will be squandered whenever you get your hands on any. Money is pure energy just like sex, which according to Steve Martin is 'the most beautiful and natural thing that money can buy'.

Other than the ultimate *why*, it is within this section that you will further define *why(s)* specific to your current needs.

Once you have completed each part of this exercise, dig out your original script.

The point of this swirling madness is to encourage you to realize that you have everything you need to create both wellbeing and success, to make you happy and to create your success, whatever that might be. Not pressuring yourself is a good way to start.

Your goals are incremental parts of a permanently transforming picture. As goals pop out at you, write them down and break them down with the complete certainty that the resources required to get you there will become available to you.

You are and always will be a permanent work in progress.

Being and becoming

The more links you can find between the, seemingly, unconnected pieces of the jigsaw puzzle you have listed, the more you will live in the present, while the complete picture reveals the **what**, the **why** and the **how**.

You are constructing a recipe, continually adding, taking away and juggling. When you can't get it to work, it's because the part you most need to throw away is the very thing to which you're attached the most, just as you find that the director's favourite scene often ends up in the deleted scenes when you switch on the audio commentary option on many DVDs.

Define your mission statement as succinctly as possible and then continue to refine it. When you have a mission statement, any choices along the way can be recognized immediately as opposed to all the debating that can go on at every step of the way.

Have a laugh! It's all about enjoying the movie.

So there's a pretty big editing job ahead of you, which is all part of a never-ending story. Don't worry, there isn't a deadline.

The greatest marriage of film and music in my opinion is *Koyaanisqatsi,* directed by Godfrey Reggio with music composed by Philip Glass and cinematography by Ron Fricke.

As a young film editor back in the 1980s, I couldn't work out how anyone could have edited the film to fit that music, or scored that music to that edit, and realized they must have at least gone backwards and forwards with a few tweaks.

They went way beyond that. The film was edited, then scored, then re-edited, then re-scored, then re-edited, then re-scored, then re-edited, then re-scored, then re-edited, then re-scored, then re-edited, then re-scored, then re-edited, then re-scored, then re-edited, then re-scored, then re-edited, then re-scored ...

*Raaargh!!! Raaargh!!! Raaargh!!! Raaargh!!! Raaargh!!!
Raaargh!!! Raaargh!!! Raaargh!!! Raaargh!!! Raaargh!!!
Raaargh!!! Raaargh!!! Raaargh!!! Raaargh!!! Raaargh!!!
Raaargh!!! Raaargh!!! Raaargh!!! Raaargh!!! Raaargh!!!
Raaargh!!! Raaargh!!! Raaargh!!! Raaargh!!! Raaargh!!!
Raaargh!!! Raaargh!!! Raaargh!!!*

Perfection...

Now, I'm not suggesting you approach any one area in your life like this.

I'm suggesting this is how you approach your life itself.

Unlike *Koyaanisqatsi*, your work is never done, but like Reggio, Fricke and Glass you can have the most deeply meaningful and amazing experience in the process as you gain understanding on how and where to apply tension and release.

Regardless how far you have delved into Exercise Infinity, the key to it all is to work out how everything you are currently doing, even with resentment, is a connected part of a work in progress that leads to what you aspire to be and do. That is how you can find inspiration from anything regardless of where it leads. So write a to-do list. And just do it.

When you live like this as you evolve from dependant to contributor, you discover that you *need* do nothing.

You are only doing what you love to do.

And as you reach the final stage of a death without regretting what you didn't do, while chuckling at the mistakes you made along the way, you no longer need to even *do* what you love, as nouns and verbs become the same thing and you become pure love itself.

Raaargh!!!

Om.

Silence.

And no need for any verbal affirmation at all.

THE END IS THE NEXT BEGINNING

And let's not concern ourselves unnecessarily with making the sequel just yet.

AFFIRMATION
I am the sum of what I am and what I aspire to be.

Hay House Titles of Related Interest

Feel Happy Now,
by Michael Neill

Fuck It,
by John Parkin

Inspiration,
by Dr Wayne W. Dyer

The Man Who Drove With His Eyes Closed,
by Barefoot Doctor

The Mindful Manifesto,
by Dr Jonty Heaversedge and Ed Halliwell

Self-Help, by
Max Kirsten

The Way of Wyrd,
by Brian Bates

All of the above are available at your
local bookshop, or may be ordered by
contacting Hay House

ABOUT THE AUTHOR

Photo: Lorenzo Agius

Keith Holden was inspired by the schoolboy phrase, 'Just do it, it's easier to apologize than ask for permission,' but found through an understanding of fair exchange that he never needed to say sorry. When an idea excited him, he simply jumped into the abyss with a **Raaargh!!!** He left school in a hurry, breathtakingly reinventing himself time and again in what reads as a fairytale book of Who's Who, while constantly searching far and wide for the treasures of understanding. What he now understands is what links all of his achievements and is available to everybody – to simply do what you love to do with anticipation and gratitude for challenge, which he simplifies further with his all-meaning mantra of **Raaargh!!!**

The **Raaargh!!!** of play is infectious. While organizing a number of events that successfully invited the audience to become the performers, he was asked by Sir Paul McCartney to put some life into his studio, and not only recorded Macca on a smoky old chainsaw, but the intoxication of **Raaargh!!!** enticed the fire brigade, alerted by the smoke detectors, to sing on the chorus.

While such yarns read well on paper, Keith says it is the jumping into the abyss itself that is the true reward, including all those endeavours that don't come off that bring with them the true gems of understanding.

He currently lives in Ibiza with his wife and two sons, and is an author, personal power trainer, business consultant, teacher and speaker.

He has something he wants to tell you.